❧SPROUT❧

selected poems
by
catarine hancock

ISBN: 9798810957409

Cover art by Catarine Hancock
Interior art by Abigail Brannon.

For permissions contact:
catarinehancock.writing@gmail.com

to my readers.

i couldn't have asked for better people to grow up with.

TRIGGER WARNING:

some poems may contain mentions of heavy themes, such as abuse, sexual assault, mental health, and body image.

please take care.

FROM ME TO YOU:

i first started writing poetry when i was 13. i was fragile and heartbroken, so convinced the world was ending because my first love had—predictably, as most first loves do—gone sour. i'd always been a reader and a writer, so it was only a matter of time before i turned to poetry. after that break-up, i finally fell into its clutches. it has been nine years, and poetry has yet to let me go. of course, i think it's pretty obvious at this point that i don't want it to.

i never intended to turn this into a career—i have no formal training outside of a few writing workshops here and there. i just have a genuine love for this artform, and i find real joy in connecting with people, with creating art that resonates with others and helps them, even slightly, to heal. growing up in the social media age and sharing so much of my soul online since i was a young girl has a lot of downfalls, but the community i've discovered, the friendships i've made, and the hearts i've impacted are not on that list. and though i did not expect to be where i am now: with an audience of 300,000, a publisher, and books in the stores i have loved since i was young, i would not change it for the world—not even the bad parts where i lost my way, became too obsessed with numbers, or stopped writing entirely. i would not have had it happen any other way.

sprout has over 200 pieces, all of which were written between the years of 2013 and 2021. some of them you may recognize from my first two collections, *the boys i've loved and the end of the world* and *how the words come* that i took down at the end of 2019. some of them were posted once years ago and never posted again. and some of them you haven't seen at all. there are poems in here that i wrote with the intention of putting into one of my books but never did.

the very first poem in this book is the exact poem i posted on july 6th, 2013, when i started my first poetry account on instagram. it is the very beginning of this long, winding path i've been on ever since, and even if it is short and cliché, i wouldn't dream of leaving it out.

as you read this collection, please keep this in mind: many of these poems are very, very old, written when i was in high school or the early years of college. i do not hate any of these pieces, but i do think some of them really show just how young i was when i wrote them. those are the poems you will read and then think, "wow, it's like a 15-year-old wrote this," and that will be because a 15-year-old did (at least, i hope that's why). i would approach a lot of these poems differently now, but i did my best to avoid revising them too much beyond fixing grammatical errors or rewording something that just didn't make sense. what would be the point of this book if i were to rewrite all the poems rather than give them to you as i wrote them all those years ago?

but even among those poems from the early years, there will be ones where you'll notice the beginnings of my poetic voice: the voice i have sharpened and honed into something recognizable all these years later. there are many pieces in here that i think are honestly really fucking good, and i am super proud of them even now. there will be lines that will jump out as something that could have fit right into *shades of lovers* or *something i fall asleep thinking about you*. many of the pieces from 2018 on were written at the same time as those collections, and may have even found a home in them had i made different choices or remembered where they hid within my notes app. as luck would have it, they have found their way into the pages of a book eventually. please know that these poems are not afterthoughts, nor do i think they are second-rate: i was simply writing a lot and not all of them could fit.

i have grown so much over the last nine years. you can see it in my writing—and i don't just mean in the way my style has evolved. you can see it in the way i stop romanticizing an abusive relationship as "right person, wrong time," and start writing about the trauma. you can see it in the way my mindsets about all my relationships change; how i, with each person i have loved, believed them to be the one i was meant to be with, and how i processed that not being true differently each time. and more than anything, you can see it in the way i write about myself.

i hope you enjoy *sprout*, aptly titled for the seed that was planted all those years ago, and all the growing and blossoming that has been happening ever since.

much love,

catarine

more by catarine hancock

shades of lovers

sometimes i fall asleep thinking about you

i gave myself the world (january 2023)

TABLE OF CONTENTS

2013

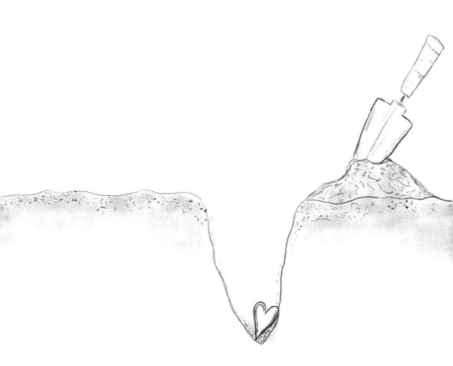

what hurts the most
is that you were mine
for so long
and now after all that time
i have to watch you be
somebody else's.

after you left,
i was told
to try to replay us
backwards
because then it's not
falling apart,
it's coming together.

i think that
us in rewind
is still just as
painful
because it begins
with you rebuilding me,
and us being happy
for a while,
until one day
you just forget about me.

but then again,
isn't that how it happened,
anyway?

i hope for your sake
that she is worth it.
that you threw away everything we had
for somebody who is worth your time.

but on the other hand,
i hope she breaks your heart over and over again
until you can't breathe,
until you are on the ground,
until you know what it feels like
to hear that the person you so dearly love
has fallen in love with somebody else.

you say you don't have a clue why you did it,
but i can't help but feel like
it was my fault more than yours,
like i didn't try hard enough
to please you,
or maybe i just didn't have enough to give.

but then i ask myself,
i loved you with everything i had,
why wasn't that enough?
why wasn't it enough
for me to pour my heart and soul out to you?
i told you some things that
people had been trying to get out of me for years,
but you got them out in a matter of days.

so i hope she is worth it,
and i also hope she destroys you,
and leaves you on the ground,
bleeding and broken and bruised,
wondering that maybe
i actually was
enough.

i have been
the hopeless dreamer.
the girl who fantasizes about a boy
who will never love her back.

i have been
the pursued and sought after.
the girl who is fantasized about
by a boy she will never love back.

but it is when these two ends meet
that it is the most painful:
when she has the world at her feet,
but the one thing she wants most,
the one boy she loves more
than anything in the whole wide world,
is out of reach.

that is when it is the most painful,
because it becomes a chase
that never ends.

it is twelve
and i don't love you
anymore

it is eleven am
and i tell him i love him
with every part of me

it is one am
he kisses me goodnight
and pulls the covers over us

it is ten am
i scroll past one of your posts
and my heart doesn't burn

it is two am
and i find myself
dreaming about you

it is nine am
we go out for breakfast
pancakes and coffee

it is three am
i awake to his soft snores
and him pulling me closer

it is eight am
he brushes my hair
as i tie my shoes

it is four am
and i sleep soundly
you never cross my mind

it is seven am
he joins me in the shower
kissing the sleep away

it is five am
i bury myself into his chest
and he smiles in his sleep

it is six am
he stirs next to me
and the birds sing outside

i used to think you'd be the one
who'd save me.

i would murmur it into your lips—
you, my saving grace,
my light at the end
of the tunnel.

eventually,
i realized you were never
my light
at all.

you weren't
the breaking of day
after a long night.

you,
you were the cruel gray
in human form.

you were the darkness
surrounding me.

"i love her,"
you said,
so i took my clock
and wound back a day,
back to when we were still happy,
but it didn't work,
because when i said,
"i love you,"
you replied,
"i love her more."

i was never a girl to say that
the boy never loved me
after a relationship ends,
because i know you loved me.
you just can't stop something from
falling apart
when someone's heart starts to beat
for somebody else.
but i know you loved me,
because although people can fake smiles,
people can never fake a look in their
eyes.

2014

i was red riding hood,
you were the big bad wolf.
i led you straight to my heart,
and you just tore it apart.

i hate to admit it dear, but i feel like a fool / trying so hard for someone who won't even play by the rules / i spent months working hard to learn this part / but you gave me one look and fucking shattered my heart / now my eyes are like ice and my words are like stone / and one day you will be left all alone / but it's what you deserve and it's what you'll get / because i'm tired of being the girl who is treated like shit

last summer, you walked with me down the railroad tracks and matched my steps with yours. you intertwined our fingers and lifted me up to balance on the metal rails. you kept me balanced; you kept me stable.

when you left, it felt like a train had barricaded right through my chest. now, i've got this gaping hole where my heart should be. instead of taking it with you, you ripped it from me and flattened it to the ground.

i can't keep my balance on the metal rails anymore.

children's games

i am tired of playing
these childhood games with you

you run too fast
and i can never reach you
for i am tired of chasing
someone who will never let
me catch them

you've always been good at hiding
but you're invisible to me
and it seems that you don't understand
the pain of losing someone and not being able
to find them again

you aren't one for following rules
and i know this because
no matter how many times i get
"he loves me"
when i pluck petals off
you always find a way for it to be
"he loves me not"

a twelve-word story

"so, what do you think about me?"
"well," he said, "i don't."

you compared me to a flower.
you told me i was as beautiful as a rose.
one day we went on a walk,
and you picked one for me.

"it's going to die,"
i said.
"but doesn't everything beautiful die, eventually?"
you countered.

little did i know,
you were talking about us.

time is everything

it's been 61 days since you last told me you loved me. 1,464 hours, or 87,840 minutes, or 5,270,400 seconds. i have never been one to keep time but i used to count the hours we talked to each other on the phone (the record was 5) and how many seconds it took for you to tell me you loved me (sometimes it was .65 seconds, but when you were feeling sad it was 3.8), and how many minutes you spent staring at me in class (one time it was a whole 12 minutes before the teacher called on you). i have been alive for 15 years, or 5,475 days, and you were a part of my life for only 102. 2,448 hours, or 146,880 minutes, or 8,812,800 seconds. i have never been one to keep time but i wanted to keep track of us. now i only keep a record of how long i go without thinking of you (5.4 minutes) and how many hours i spend crying because you're gone (so far: 73). i have never been one to keep time but i wanted to count how many days (64) i was in love with you and now i have to count how many days i'm going to hurt because you left (forever).

she was always reading:
a sign of intelligence, one might say.
but in reality,

she was only reading
because these stories of
warriors and kingdoms,
princesses and dragons,
metaphors and cancer,

were a thousand times better
than what lay off the pages.

i think you might have ruined me (and you don't even know it)

ever since the beginning, i knew i'd do anything for you. i knew i would do anything to see you smile; your smile was so beautiful. i knew i would break my own bones trying to please you, hammer nails into my heart, peel away the cracked pieces and dump them, bloody, into your hands even if you didn't ask for them (the fact that you'd hold them for a moment was a privilege in and of itself). it was a drunk obsession, i stumbled after you like i was a lost dog hoping that someone, someone would just take me home, i swayed under your gaze even if you never let it rest on me for long. i clung to every part of you, all the parts you never gave me, all the parts i knew i could have loved–the parts i did love even though you never asked me to. you were the source of all my pain and yet i wanted you to end it all. i longed for you to take away the pain, you were the band-aid and the bullet, the gun at the soldier's head who was fatally shot seconds before. the one thing that kills me is the one thing that saves me: and it's you, you, you. it's always been you.

i didn't know you'd regret me that much

your eyes are full of anger,
your sneer is full of hate.

you never seemed to understand
you have to watch the steps you take.

your methods of forgetting
are far less than futile

you know you can't erase
how you felt when you saw me smile.

so call me what you please,
say i was a mistake

but you can't always reverse
what you once thought was fate.

the healing process

the strangest thing about forgetting is what you still remember. little bits and pieces stay behind, while what you think would never leave you, disappears from your memory.

i can't remember your face. i can't hear your voice buzzing in my ear like it used to.

i can remember the color of your kitchen countertops; brown granite, like your eyes, but even then i can't recall the exact shade of your irises. i can remember how your house smelled on a sunday, but i don't even remember the scent of your cologne.

there is a small clip of your laugh in the back of my mind. i'll reach in and press play sometimes, but each time it becomes more and more muffled, the audio skipping, skipping, skipping. i remember every callous on your hand, every line, but i can't remember the way your lips curved up in a smile.

i can't remember your face, and every day, a little piece of you floats off and leaves me like you did.

i'll trace the outline of my collarbone like you used to in hopes to see your ghost sometimes. but nothing comes.

i can't remember your face, because the mind blocks out traumatic events, traumatic people. my mind has blocked out your face, and maybe that's the most traumatic thing of all.

as the water pulls me down,
i remember how you told me
i could swim.

you planted your words in my heart
and with every passing day
they blossomed.
the stems wrapped around my heart
and the buds poked through my ribcage.
you nurtured them until
i had leaves in my brain
and roots in my stomach.

when you left
the flowers within me died and sagged
on their perches:
a constant reminder
to never let love consume me
again.

the definition of a word is the way it slips from your lips / how it builds in your throat before you realize it / how your eyes water before you stop biting your tongue / the definition of a word is the wat it slams through their chest and crushes their heart / the definition of a word is how sorry you are that you broke them

i always knew
you'd be a chapter in my story

i just didn't know
you'd be the one
to throw everything
off balance

you're the chapter
that causes the main character
so much fucking pain

you are the conflict
the villain and antagonist

i hate you so much
it makes my hands quiver
when i turn the pages
through our little chapter

as my teardrops
stain the paper
and smear the ink

turning our story
into messy ruin
just like you did
to my heart

-i hope i find a resolution to you

i was walking down
the street today
and it smelled like
your house on a sunday—

your dad's cigarettes
and cleaning supplies

i could almost feel
the cigarette smoke
in my lungs and
the smell of acidic chemicals
burning my nose

so many toxic things
in your house already

why not just add another
and give it
your name?

your fingerprints left burns
all over my body

i used to think
that was a sign
of the intensity
of your love

but you left me with scars
and a body crumbling
to nothing
but ash

i hope the embers
burn your feet
as you walk away
from me

i used to say
i could see stars
in your eyes

they say it takes
a million years
before we know
if a star is dead

so how will i know
what you're really feeling
until it's too late?

2015

here's the reason why i left you

we are a fire:
we are flaming
with red-hot passion
and we burn
and burn
and burn

we are a fire:
it only took a spark
for us to light a wildfire
and we burn
and burn
and burn

we are a fire:
we need oxygen to live
but we are too close to breathe
and we burn
and burn
and burn
out.

he used to love me, i think

he wasn't someone i saw coming, but they never are, are they? he was the most beautiful mistake i ever made, if you consider it a mistake. but i never thought it was. merely the wrong place and wrong time. people would roll their eyes and shake their heads, but we never asked for their approval. to us, it was all right. every last moment. he was a compilation of all the beautiful things in the world that had strings attached. he was a summer thunderstorm with the fallen tree that blocks your driveway. he was the stars in the sky that died centuries ago. he was the high and the low, the beautiful fire and its scorching burn. i wrote poetry about him for months after he was gone and with every word a wound reopened but the pain reminds me of him so i keep writing. i can't stop. won't stop. i used to not be able to write, but now i can't stop and it hurts so much. he hurts so much, but he is so beautiful. i will never be able to say he is not beautiful, and that is the saddest thing of all. he stopped calling me beautiful a long time ago, the words left his mind, slipped off his tongue in another conversation with someone who means more than me now. the most painful thing about love is that somebody has to stop eventually and it's never going to be you. it will always be them. they will be empty before you're even at halfway and you'll be left with gallons of love and nowhere to put them. the obvious thing to do would be to love yourself, but your eyesight is clouded with agony, so you can't see what's two feet in front of you anymore. so instead it drips out, useless, wasted on meaningless kisses in the middle of the night behind your neighbor's garage, pointless promises and grasping hands under sheets that aren't clean, metaphorically, or literally. i still write about him, even now. it's been months since he told me he didn't love me anymore and i still write about him as if he does. i used to not be able to write but now i can't stop and he is so beautiful, and even now that's all i see and that is the saddest thing of all.

tomorrow

the sink in the kitchen won't stop dripping. when i sit on the living room couch i can hear it over the hum of the television and i think i've told you to fix it four times. every time you smile and tell me you will tomorrow. that's what you've always said. "i'll mop the floor-- tomorrow. i'll mow the yard-- tomorrow. i'll stop you from crying-- tomorrow." i'm beginning to think that you are just an endless closet of throw-away promises and old shoes that you used to wear when you liked to chase me. once you caught me, you took them off and never put them back on because you knew you'd never need to. they sit in the closet next to a pile of tomorrows and i don't let you see me cry anymore. you've long since forgotten how to make me stop.

the sink in the kitchen keeps dripping and it keeps me up at night. i once believed that our house was too small for the size of us but i can feel the cold seeping in from the corners because this house is empty. it has cobwebs inside the cupboards and dust bunnies under the bed; they keep our secrets company. i never told you how afraid i was to lose you-- i tried, and you shook your head and said, "tomorrow." tomorrow. tomorrow.

maybe tomorrow will be better, i tell myself, maybe tomorrow you will clean the gutters, maybe tomorrow you will fix the sink, maybe tomorrow you will love me again; i've been told that you begin to develop the habits of the ones you love and i've started adding my tomorrows to the pile in the closet. they've covered your old shoes and you've forgotten what it was like to love me, and the sink in the kitchen won't stop dripping but it still works. you still come home every day. you barely talk to me, but you still come home.

i look at you, and i think about tomorrow. tomorrow. tomorrow. maybe tomorrow you won't come home. maybe i hope, deep down, that tomorrow, you won't. maybe eventually, these will be tomorrows that i won't add to the pile in the closet. there are pictures of us hung above the fireplace, and the mantle is covered with dust. the sink in the kitchen still drips, but i say, "i love you," anyway. i hope you'll love me too, tomorrow.

the boys i've loved and the end of the world #1

"the world is ending, you know."

he looks at me through tired eyes as i say it. "is that why you're here?"

i shrug. "i guess." he takes a pack of cigarettes out of his pocket and smiles when i raise my eyebrows. "i didn't know you smoke, now," i say.

"i don't," he explains as he places one between his lips, "but the world is ending. can't get lung cancer in twelve days."

i chuckle, watch him take his first drag from his first cigarette. he coughs, and smiles at me. "i loved you, you do know that, right?"

"yeah, yeah, i know," i reply, and he takes a longer drag this time.

"you were important… an important lesson, i think."

"how so?"

"we were too young, too stupid. we were incapable of fixing the mess we'd made with our own two hands. only time could do that."

he nods, smoke filtering from his parted lips. the moon turns his black hair to a silvery blue, and i am almost caught up in how beautiful he could be, sometimes.

"how many times did you fall in love with her before you realized she would never give you what you wanted?" i ask, and he blinks, surprised by the question.

"the same goes for you," he counters, "but with me instead." there is a comfortable silence. "twice," i say, finally, "what about you?"

"twice. and it was always after you. it was always what ruined us, again and again."

i think about this as he finishes his cigarette. "sometimes, i wonder if we could have made it. if we weren't so young," i tell him.

he nods his head, smiles. "yeah, sometimes i think about that too."

the boys i've loved and the end of the world #2

"they say it's a solar flare, the biggest one they've ever seen,"
he says with a sigh.

"are you scared?" i ask.

he runs his hand through his hair. "i don't think so.
it's inevitable, right?"

"sure. but aren't you scared of death?"

"why would i be? sometimes i try to get there early." there is a
smile on his face, but the weight of his words is still so heavy in
the air.

"you never take anything seriously," i mumble, more to myself
than anything, but he hears me.

"sure i do. i took you seriously."

"but you left."

"still. you were my favorite thing," he says, quietly, as if he is
afraid of what i'll do when i hear it.

"then why did you push me away? after all that time, all those
memories, and you just… told me to leave."

"i was made up of a million mistakes already. i didn't want you
to become another one."

"but i did anyway, didn't i?" i press.

"not exactly. because i let you go, you met him, and you were
happy. and even though it wasn't with me, it was… it was
something, you know? something to feel good about."

"so in a way, it was always about me, wasn't it?"

he looks at me then, and his blue eyes are sad, like they always are.

"until the end," he says.

the boys i've loved and the end of the world #3

"do you think it'll be quick or slow?" i ask him. we are sitting on a bench, separate sides, but it is comfortable.

"i'm not sure. do you think it'll hurt?" he responds, looking at me with eyes that have never been anything but kind.

"i'm sorry if i ever hurt you," i blurt out, because i feel like i need to say it.

"you didn't break my heart," he says honestly, "we fell apart in a way that didn't let you."

"i wouldn't have even if i'd had the chance." there is a pause, and the trees cast shadows over us. "you taught me how to love myself, i hope you know that."

he smiles. "i didn't teach you anything. you learned how to on your own."

"it was because of you, though." i pause, then ask, "do you tell her that you love her every chance you get?"

"of course." he fumbles with his hands. "there's only so many chances left to say it, anyway."

we sit together, and i tuck my knees into my chest and rest my chin on them. he watches the sky, frowning, and i want to say that he is too good to be wiped out by a solar flare, but i don't.

instead i say, "i'm so fucking scared."

he reaches over and rests his hand on my shoulder. "me too."

"i learned from you that love doesn't always have to end nasty. sometimes, it just stops."

he nods, agreeing, and squeezes my shoulder once.

"maybe that'll be how the world ends," he suggests, "it won't end terribly. it'll just stop."

the boys i've loved and the end of the world #4

"it's going to consume the earth. a giant light ball, and it's going to swallow the earth whole."

we are walking, in his town, a town i've never been to until now. our arms swing side by side, sometimes brushing, and the sun is beaming calmly down on us. "i still find it hard to believe that the sun shining on us now, is the same sun that will kill everyone and obliterate the planet in three days," i say with a slight laugh.

"i still find it hard to believe that i'll never get a chance to marry you," he responds, and i hit his arm, but i am laughing and so is he.

"maybe in heaven, you will," i giggle, and he rolls his eyes.

"please, we both know it's not real," he scoffs, but he looks at me and his eyes are scared. i know, that if i could see mine in a mirror, they would be, too. he grabs my arm, stopping us. "tell me, was it always the distance that pushed you away?"

i nod, and my chest feels heavy. "of course it was. it's always the distance, isn't it?" i sigh, knowing that every promise i made to him, won't matter in three days' time. "i wish it hadn't been there."

he draws me closer, wraps his arms around me, and i let him. i will never feel them again after today. "i wanted to give you the world," he whispers, "ever since i first saw you, i wanted to give you everything i had. you were it for me."

i bury my face into his chest and say nothing. but he knows i feel the same. he's always known, and he'll go to his death knowing it, crumbled to ash by the broken sun.

"i hope he knows how lucky he is to be loved by you," he murmurs into my hair, "i hope he knows that he's holding a star brighter than the sun in his arms."

i am crying now, and i clutch his jacket tight. "i have never been sorrier about anything," i confess, "there is nothing that hurts more than knowing we will never get a chance."

"if heaven is real, please promise you will find me there." he cups my face in his hands, forcing me to look up at him.

"i promise. i promise, i promise, i promise."

with a sigh, he presses his lips to my forehead. "good. i cannot bear the distance any longer."

the boys i've loved and the end of the world #5

"i can't believe i'm going to die young," he says, his arms folded around me, "i thought i was going to grow old and have kids and pay taxes."

"nothing ever turns out as planned, does it?" i say, tired. we are waiting, tangled up in sheets and blankets and our own bodies.

"i guess, spending the end of the world with you isn't so bad," he jokes, and i kiss him. he is warm and tastes like sunlight, if it had a flavor, the kind that didn't destroy planets and burn everything to nothing.

"what if we're already dead, and we don't know it. it happened so fast that we didn't even feel anything, so this is heaven."

"what if, you're just crazy." i raise my hand to hit him, but he catches it and holds it in his own as he kisses me again. "i thought we'd have more time," he says sadly.

outside, the sky is glowing. i look at the clock and it's eleven at night. the end is coming.

"i thought we would, too." he holds me tighter, and we watch the sky. it's beautiful, and i smile.

the wind starts to beat against the walls, and i can feel it getting closer, ripping up the ground.

"i always hoped we would last," he yells over it all, and he is crying, and so am i, but even now he is beautiful, and i want to kiss him.

"we lasted until the end of the world, didn't we?" i shout, and he laughs, a carefree, happy sound, and i cherish it, knowing i may never hear it again.

the wind grows louder and the glass in the windows start to crack. i kiss him, hard, and he pulls the blanket over us.

for a moment, there is nothing but the two of us and the sound of our heartbeats.

then, there is nothing but light.

the boys i've loved and the end of the world, epilogue

i wonder if they will all be here, the boys i've loved, wherever we are now.

i wonder if i will see the first. he took so much from me that i will never get back. but he gave me so much too; things i will never get from anyone else. a first love. my heart, broken for the first time. a heap of common sense. i hope he will be here. he has a beautiful smile. i hope he will stop smoking, even if you can't get lung cancer in heaven. i don't want him to accidentally burn it down. that sounds like something he would do.

if the second is here, i hope his sadness is gone, destroyed back on earth with everything else. he has been hurt so much. he doesn't deserve it anymore. i know we will never get another chance, not at love, anyways. but perhaps we can rebuild something else: our friendship. who knows? time is endless here.

i know the third will be here, waiting to greet everyone else with open arms. i hope she is there, too, holding his hand. he has a heart of gold, and i am glad he walked away from me without it completely shattered. even now, i would put him before me, simply because i know he is a better person than i have ever been. so if it were between the two of us getting into wherever our afterlife is, i would tell him to go.

the fourth never believed, but then again, neither did i, and yet it is white all around me and i am certain this is not hell. i only hope he is here, too. i promised i would find him. i can only hope i do, and i can only hope we finally get a chance, without miles between us and scattered internet connection being the only thing holding us together.

i think about the fifth, how little time we had. but we have all the time we want here. so much, that one day, we may get bored, as young people do. but i do not want to think about the sad ending now. we have the rest of our lives ahead of us, even if it isn't the way we planned. but things never turn out as planned, do they?

there! i can see them all… they are waiting for me. i must go to them. the air is crisp and the sky is bright. everything is peaceful. the sun will not hurt us here.

here, we have all the chances we need.

metaphorically speaking

it's impossible to describe exactly how you made me feel but you were like a cold drink on an eighty-degree day, you were like freshly shaven legs, you were like feeling the beach sand in between your toes and the waves lapping against your shins, you were refreshing, renewing. i don't know how to describe exactly how it felt when you touched me but it was like a hot towel pressed against my skin, it was like the slightest of electrocutions, it was like feeling the warm sun beat down on your back, it was intense, warm. i could never explain exactly how it felt when you broke me but it felt like stubbing your foot on the corner of the table a dozen times over, it was like having a cough and not being able to swallow your breath, it was like chopping vegetables and cutting your finger, it was sudden, painful. i don't know to describe any of this properly but i guess i'm doing the best i can given the fact that when you left you took all of me with you.

losing you

time is everything and we are running out of it--*tick tick tick*--my eyes twitch and my hands tremble but shaking doesn't bring you back--*won't bring you back*--shaking only rattles our bones and cracks our fingers--*crack crack crack*--and i cry for you--*please please please stay stay stay* with me--but you can't--*you can't-- we* can't anymore--time is everything and we are running out of it--*tick tick*--slipping through our fingers like sand and blowing away with the wind--*gone gone gone--you are gone gone gone* and i reach in the dark for you but i can't see your eyes any more *where are you*--you *promised--lies lies lies*--time is everything and we are running out of it--*tick*

to be loved by me

falling in love with a writer means they will describe every inch of you in such intricate detail it will make you think they've seen more of you than you have. it means you'll wake up to long text messages sent at 1:13 am when you were fast asleep, but they were awake writing about what they hoped you were dreaming about. it means they'll sneak love notes into your pockets, trace words with their fingers along your collarbone. it means they'll take your promises seriously, and scribble them down in their journal to read over every time they feel a little down.

falling in love with a writer means you will never realize how powerful words are until they tell you they love you without actually saying it.

falling in love with a writer means reading everything they write, even if they've hit a block and all of their sentences are tangled up in knots. it means finding yourself reading poetry late at night when you can't sleep. it means understanding that they are always writing, narrating, creating in their heads, making everything you do sound beautiful to them.

and if anyone else were to be listening to their thoughts, they'd think you were beautiful, too.

2016

eclipse

we looked at each other like
we were the sun and the moon
locked in a gravitational war,
bound to cross and bound to
break apart.

to you,
i was the entire night sky.
to me,
you were just another
forlorn stargazer.

but you looked at me like
i was your whole universe.
i cried because i was
full of dead stars and broken debris,
but you still called me
beautiful.

you were the flaming meteor
about to send me up in smoke
but i kissed you anyway.

there's a burning crater on my lips
from your touch and
i think i may always be in love
with you.

we looked at each other like
we were the sun and the moon
and we knew we'd only eclipse for so long.

we knew all along that
soon we would be apart,
just waiting for gravity to
bring us back together
again.

you're the only one who doesn't haunt me

i think i saw you in my dreams, my dear,
it brought us back to the time,
when life was far less complicated,
and you would say, "you're mine."

you were by far the only one i loved,
but that was way back then,
for we walked on a long old rope
that was paper, paper thin.

it snapped and sent us falling down,
i felt you slip away from me,
but that's okay, for when i landed,
there was something beautiful to see.

i saw the gold around my feet
and the darkness up above:
sometimes the key to joy
is falling out of love.

i think i saw you in my dreams, my dear,
and i learned a thing or two,
i have a soulmate, he's there somewhere,
but that soulmate isn't you.

for the girls with the frizzy hair and bitten nails and the boys with bushy eyebrows and marionette limbs:

1. there will be the kids with perfect skin and white smiles and flawless bodies. do not be scared of them. often the "prettiest" people are the most hurt inside.
2. find a home away from home for yourself, whether it be the gym floor, the computer lab, or the auditorium stage. you will need one.
3. let your heart get broken. you have to learn how to breathe with pieces of your heart piercing your lungs. trust somebody you shouldn't. make a bad decision. but always learn from your mistakes. too many wrong moves will kill you.
4. there will always be somebody out to get you. don't let them.
5. in every school, there is one teacher that you will connect with more than any other. cherish that bond, because it only comes once, and you only have so much time.
6. don't wear that dress if it doesn't feel right. don't wear that shirt if you don't actually like it. don't do anything you don't want to do for the sake of staying with the trends.
7. for the girls: if somebody touches you in a way you don't like, don't be afraid to fight back. you are not weak. you are not an object. make sure they, and you, know that. make sure your fellow girls know their worth, too, and do not contribute to the degradation of it.
8. for the boys: if you see a girl in trouble, help her. make sure she doesn't go into that bedroom alone with him while she's drunk. stand up for her if she's being harassed. if you see something but can't do anything yourself; tell somebody. call the police. protect girls and educate your fellow boys on how to treat them.

9. watch the news. read the paper. engage in discussion. know about politics and what's going on in the world. in times like these, it's no longer alright to not care about things; in fact, it could be harmful.

10. people will die. people you know, people your peers know. car wrecks, drugs, suicides, gun violence: they will all take people you walk those halls with. so, that being said: if you love somebody, tell them. if you think somebody may need a friend, be that friend. you don't want to be stuck in the aftermath of a tragedy, thinking, "oh, if only i'd said this. if only i'd done this."

11. there will be days where you look in the mirror and want to remold your body like clay, days where you may not even want to get out of bed. on those days, it's okay to cry, to want to be different. but the next morning, remind yourself; you will be okay, you will be okay, you will be okay.

an excerpt (#1)

and he looks at her so delicately, with such a twinkle in his eyes, that i cannot help but let out a soft, "oh," from between my lips.

"hmm?" he doesn't take his eyes off of the girl asleep on his lap, her dark hair falling across her shoulders and face, and her hand resting gently on his.

"you're in love with her, aren't you?"

he smiles and tears his gaze from her to meet mine. "of course i am, and you aren't?" there isn't a trace of sarcasm or lightness in his voice; he is completely serious— '*and you aren't*'?

"well, no, but i suppose i can see why you are," i reply, and he chuckles dryly.

"you suppose you can see why..." he murmurs, more to himself than anything, and lowers his eyes so that he can once again stare adoringly at the sleeping girl.

"she is beautiful," i say, in an effort to redeem myself, "and she's very kind, and intelligent."

"oh, i know," he cuts me off, "but she's so much more." he smiles and twines a strand of her hair around his fingers. "she's someone that you never know you need, until you meet her. and she's someone you never know you won't be able to live without, until you lose her."

"does she love you, too?" i have to know, i realize. surely, she loves him back. she must.

"in her own little way, she does." he frowns. they have problems when it comes to this; it's obvious. "but i know she's loved others, too." his eyes darken. "loves others, i mean."

"she does love him, and i'm sure it hurts you."

he knows who i'm talking about when i say 'him.' he sighs, and shrugs. "it does, but only a little bit. he won't have her in the end."

it's an awfully arrogant thing to say, i think; *'he won't have her in the end'*. he's so sure she'll be his. "i don't understand. how can you be so sure?"

"you never saw us together," he says simply, as if it were obvious, "not when we were really together. if you did, you would understand." his eyes cloud as he remembers. "oh, us, together... together, we could take over the world."

an excerpt (#2)

"did he break your heart?"

"no, i don't think so," she answers, but she sounds uncertain. the question has made her reconsider. after a moment, she says, "he hurt me. there's no use in denying that."

he looks at her. "how badly?"

she shrugs, looks down at her shoes. "enough to make me cry. enough… just enough. he hurt me enough."

he blinks and rolls a lighter between his fingers. he's not a smoker, but she is, and he thought he would give it to her, maybe. just to try and get through to her. "did you love him?"

she laughs at this, and tucks her knees into her chest, "nah, not even close." she sighs, "i could have though, i think." her eyes darken, "if he'd given me the chance to."

he's unsure of how to respond, so he hands her the lighter. "it's for you," he mumbles, and she smiles for a fleeting second, takes it from his grasp, and then hands it back.

"no thanks," she says, and then explains, "i'm trying to quit. i wanna go somewhere, live a long time. can't do that if i smoke, ya know?"

"yeah, i know, i just thought–"

she squeezes his hand, "i know what you thought, and it's sweet. you're sweet." he smiles, and for a moment, she smiles back at him. then it slides off her face, and he waits for her to speak.

"it just, it just sucks getting fucked over, ya know?" she runs a hand through her hair, "like, he was so important. it wasn't that i wanted to date him or any of that, but he was just important. he used to say that i was important too, and that's what hurts the most, i think. the fact that he just randomly decided that i wasn't anymore."

he opens his mouth, but she keeps going.

"so i guess, in a way, he might have broken my heart. not enough for me to feel it for a long time, but just enough to remind me that he meant something to me, and he fucking walked away."

"he hurt you enough," he echoes her previous words.

"yeah, yeah," she wipes a tear away with the palm of her hand, "he hurt me enough."

an excerpt (#3)

"tell me, why do we romanticize pain?" he asks, staring not at her, but up at the clouds.

"i think we do it to understand it better," she answers, and he frowns.

"how does that work? there's nothing beautiful about pain. beautiful things can come out of pain, sure, but pain in and of itself is not beautiful."

"maybe... maybe, we do it because it's the only way we can stand to think about it. we, as humans, we want to reject the ugly things in life. take 'ugly' with a grain of salt, though, because in the past, those we have rejected for being 'ugly' weren't ugly at all. but our brains are limited, and easily corrupted by preconceived ideas. so maybe, because we can't get rid of pain, we try and make it more glamorous, so we won't just shut it away. because part of coping with pain in a healthy way is being open about it."

he laughs and looks at her. "you're very smart, you know that?"

she feels herself blushing. "i guess."

he touches her hand, briefly. "it doesn't make it right, does it?" he inquires, "it's not good to make pain seem beautiful. it makes people think being in pain is good, that it makes you beautiful. so really, by trying to understand it better, we really aren't understanding it at all."

"well, nobody wants to be sad, but everyone wants to be beautiful, whatever their definition of 'beautiful' may be. so if you're sad, romanticizing it may be the only way to feel beautiful."

"but it's toxic. it hurts you. if you become so convinced that your pain is beautiful, that it's art, then you never want to be happy."

"i wouldn't say that." she squints her eyes, pursing her lips, "everyone wants to be happy. but i think... i think people just settle, after a while. they get tired. so they rest assured knowing that people on social media find their sadness attractive and romantic, so they still feel beautiful, in a sense."

"is that what you think?"

"yeah, it is," she says, "maybe i'm wrong, though. i don't know. i've just never really understood why people think kissing scars is going to make them go away. or that saying suicide is beautiful is going to make it stop."

"because everyone wants to be beautiful, right?" he touches her hand, again.

"yeah," she chuckles, sadly, "right."

galactic

you called me a galaxy.
you played connect the dots with
the freckles on my arms
and called them constellations.
you told me i had stars in my eyes
and celestial matter in my veins.
you said falling for me was like
falling into a black hole:
endless, exhilarating.

but your words struck me like meteors,
and your glare burned me like the sun.
it occurred to me that, like the moon,
you were only with me at night,
and i never saw all of who you were.
we ended like a supernova,
in an explosion that was slow and fast
at the same time.

a princess poem

cinderella, cinderella,
she lived her life in shame.
it wasn't until a man saved her
that she finally tasted fame.

"rapunzel, rapunzel,
just let down your hair!"
Prince Charming is upset,
he actually needs her help, how unfair!

belle, belle,
would have been content with her books,
but she had to be kidnapped
to change a man's looks.

aurora, aurora,
what kind of curse is this?
that the only cure is the touch
of an unknown man's lips?

snow white, snow white,
what a housewife you are.
you're much more than cleaning,
this role is so subpar.

princesses, princesses,
what a repetitive story.
all about needing a man
to achieve glory.

women, women,
you're not alone.
no longer do you need a king:
you can be a queen on your own.

as a woman

i wrote once in a poem
that women are hostages
of expectation.

it has been almost three years
since those words left
my mind and bled onto paper

and i have yet to find
them false.

society is full of contradictions
and it is built this way so we
are always stuck on the ground.
we do one thing we think they want
but then they tell us they want another,
and it goes in a cycle. we can never
climb over the ledge.

they tell us to wear makeup,
so we dab foundation onto
our skin and brush on silky
highlighters and mascara,
only for them to tell us
it's too much-- they like it
natural.

so we wipe off the makeup,
walk out onto the streets
with a face that has undereye bags,
splotches of acne, uneven skin,
and then they tell us that
we look sloppy—we should try
harder.
we are taught through the media
that women are sexual creatures.
everywhere we go, we see the pictures
and hear the songs.

if we refuse to be sexual, we are ridiculed.
if we harness it for ourselves, we are crucified.
if we don't put out, we are hated.
if we do and are proud, we are hated even more.

men want to see us naked and submissive,
naked and insecure
naked and silent,
not naked and dominant,
naked and confident,
naked and loud.

when a woman posts
a half-naked photo
because she wants to,
she will be ridiculed by the same
men who watch lesbian porn
in between harassing women
online for taking control of
the sexuality they demanded
we have.

they tell us to love ourselves
but then they bash us for it
if we aren't what they want,
if loving ourselves means going against
everything they've told us.

so women find themselves trapped--
trapped because every move
is a wrong one.

"wear makeup,
but not because you want to."

"be sexual,
but don't be proud of it."

"love yourself,

but not too much.

you may get away from us then."

what ruined us (or maybe you just didn't care)

i loved you
vibrantly. entirely.
constantly.
like there was nothing
else in the world
worth loving.
like you were the end.

i loved you
angrily. maddeningly.
yearningly.
like the distance
was the only problem.
like it was the only reason
you weren't always there.

i loved you
sadly. delicately.
wishfully.
like you were breaking me
but i still wouldn't blame you.
like your promises were real
and you actually believed in them.

you loved me
casually. easily.
partially.
like i didn't mean as much
as you said i did.
like you didn't love me
at all.

so this is how it feels to have someone give up on you

i remember when you first
told me you loved me,
and you held my hands in yours and
whispered it again and again
in my ear until i was in tears,
and my heart was flying out of my chest.

there is so much time and space
between us now and i do not know
how to make it go away.
i do not like the distance in the slightest
but i cannot figure out how
to make it disappear. i don't think
you ever wanted to leave, really.
but you have always been impatient.

i spend my time counting out
the minutes and seconds and days
and hours that have passed since
you've gone.
i know you are with her;
it hurts me so, but i cannot forget it,
no matter how hard i try.
it's funny how the most painful memories
are the ones that stay.

she is not a poet like i am.
she cannot make you sound beautiful
the way i do, she cannot write you
love poems that can be framed
and put on the wall.
i hope she doesn't love you as well as i did,
as well as i do, so maybe you will realize, me.
after all this time.

one time, you told me you wanted
to marry me. i think you still do,
deep down. i hope she hears it when

you say my name. "i don't love her, anymore,"
you tell her, but all she hears is,

"i do, i do."

why i cried when you first told me you loved me

i am afraid. i am afraid of drowning in the depths of your blue irises but i am also afraid that if i do not take the plunge i will feel you slip away from me like sand between my fingers. i am afraid to let you light a fire in my heart but i am even more afraid that if you do not i will slowly melt from the inside out for it has been too long since someone with warm hands has touched me. i am afraid to love you but i am also afraid to lose you and to do one will prevent the other from happening at least for some time. i am afraid of being struck by the electricity in your fingertips i am afraid of being blown away by the power behind your words i am afraid of dying because of you. i am afraid of everything and nothing all at the same time because you make me quake with uncertainty and terror but you make my blood rush and my heart pound in the most delightful of ways because with you i think i am okay and i do not know if you feel the same. *i am afraid i am afraid i am afraid* because it is you who holds my heart in their palms and it is you who sometimes trips over their own feet and it is not me who decides when i am to be broken. i am afraid because you have the power to give me everything and take it all away at the same time.

ten things that told me you never loved me at all

1. four months in, i asked you, "do you know how i like my coffee?" and you frowned. "no," you said, "but i know when your birthday is. i remember the big things." but you forgot that i loved you, and that was the biggest thing of all.

2. after you first kissed me, you shrugged. i never understood the shrug until now. i was never more than a shrug to you, in the grand scheme of things, just a moment of 'i guess,' and to me, you were the epitome of 'absolutely.'

3. when i first said "i love you," you hesitated. you always hesitated with me. it was never the nervous kind, or the shocked kind. it was always the kind of hesitation when you don't mean what you're about to say. the kind of hesitation before you lie.

4. one time, i said, "baby, i'll always wait for you. if you ever have to leave, i'll wait for you to come back." you said, "okay."

5. when you left, you told me, "i never wanted it to be this deep. i never wanted you to fall in love with me. this wasn't supposed to be serious." i spent the next three months wondering if i was the problem; maybe i confused infatuation with love. but now i know that deep down, you were just angry at yourself. because you were telling the truth: you didn't want it to be this deep, but you let it happen. and knowing this doesn't make it any less painful.

6. you never once apologized for breaking my heart. not while you were leaving, when i was sobbing and telling you that breaking my heart was, in fact, exactly what you were doing. nor did you apologize in the months that followed. even now, i wait to hear from you. not because i still love you, but because i just want to know that you finally understand what you did. i don't think you ever will.

7. you never wanted to post pictures of me. or with me, frankly. you never brought me to any parties. when we hung out, it was always just us. maybe you were ashamed of yourself, but i always just thought i was an embarrassment. you never did anything to reassure me that i wasn't.

8. a month later, i texted you. "i just want to know if you're sorry. at all. even just the slightest bit. all i want is closure." you read it, and didn't reply, and that gave me my answer.

9. i saw you, once, at a party. alone. we spoke, briefly, and i said, "you let me waste half of a year on you. you could have stopped it before i was too far gone." you sighed, "i know i could've." i remember feeling so angry, so hateful. "then why didn't you?" and you looked at your feet, "i just kept hoping that i would feel something. anything. for your sake," and then you looked at me as if that equated to an apology. "you're full of shit," i spat, "you're not sorry. you loved the attention, and i bet you loved knowing that i was crying over you for months." you ran your hands through your hair, but you didn't say i was wrong.

10. four months in, i asked you, "do you know how i like my coffee?" and you frowned. "no," you said, "but i know when your birthday is." three weeks later, my birthday passed. and you forgot.

2017

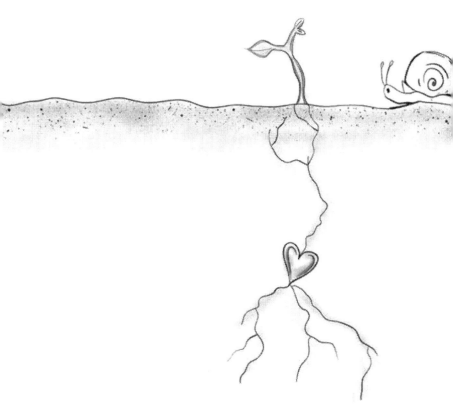

library of lovers

in my mind
sits a library.
the books in it
hold very special
tales; romances,
my romances.

sometimes i find
myself sitting in the library
when i'm tired or lonely,
brushing my fingers over
dusty books that have long
been closed.
sometimes, i even reach up
and pull one from the shelf,
open it and escape to what once was.

there are small books that
take all of an hour to read:
they ended shortly, abruptly, even,
and they either left me wishing
it was longer,
or glad that it ended when it did.
there are large books,
the ones that take days or weeks
to get through.
these are the books i grew
attached to, and i was sad
when they came to an end.
at least, unlike the shorter ones,
they had time to develop,
and they didn't leave me
thirsty for more.
then there are the series,
the stories that were too long
and too intricate to be held within
one book.

these are the ones that i found myself
unable to put down, even when
they were finished.
the ones that i had been reading
for so long i didn't know what to do
once they were done.

there are many books
i have yet to read in this library.
there are some books i may
never open, depending on
where life takes me,
and some books
i never finished reading,
and put back on the shelf
before they ended.
 i have my favorites,
the ones i like to
skim through every
once in a while.

and then i have the
book i am reading now.

i have read many books
that have had sad endings,
or angry endings,
and ones that have hardly
had an ending at all.
i hope that for once,
this book ends happily,
and when it is finished,
i never have to read another
book again.

the aftermath

people say it's possible
to die from a broken heart.
before you,
i didn't believe it.

but then you left.

and suddenly,
i couldn't breathe.
i found myself
sitting in the shower,
choking on boiling water
and watching my skin
blister red.

suddenly,
there was a gaping
hole in my chest.
i would find myself
hunched over the toilet
and heaving up what
little food i could manage
to eat.

there were days
where i could hardly
manage to get out of bed.
when my limbs would shake
and i would have to think
about each step before
i took it.

i still don't believe
that it's possible to die
from a broken heart.
but i know now
that it's possible to feel
like you are.

conclusive

you ask
is the reason
you're so sad nowadays
because of me

i say
of course not

but i can feel the lie
licking at the back of my teeth

you ask
then why do you look
like you're about to cry
whenever you glance my way

i say
i don't know what
you're talking about

and i try to hide
that the tears are there
even now

you say
i may be pathetic
but i've never been blind

i look away and i confess
i don't think
we were ever meant
to fall in love

you stop speaking
and for a few minutes
we just sit
you smoke a cigarette
and i bite my nails

then you say
if we were never
meant to fall in love
then why did we

i don't have
an answer for this
but you take my silence
as one and let the smoke
float around us before you
speak again

i think we were meant
to fall in love but maybe
we weren't meant to fall
in love for forever

i say
this is heartbreaking

you say
well at least now
we know why it is

i've spent so long chasing after someone who doesn't care
my lungs crack like the ground in a drought
and i find it harder to
breathe
and breathe
and breathe

i have spent so long waiting for you
and i'm just now realizing that
you aren't coming back--
                    (why would you? i am so
                    small and unimportant)

in retrospect i may have been
a little too hopeful
considering you never gave a shit about me
                    (i just wanted you to so badly)

so i suck in mouthfuls of dust and swallow the sand
that's gathered under my tongue while i've stood here
not loving
not living
not breathing
for anyone else but you
                    (it's a wonder i didn't crumble to nothing)

a series of short poems on the boys who love(d) me

1. you were my first everything
   and you ruined me you are
   why i have doubts about boys
   when they tell me they love me
   but we were young and stupid
   i've finally forgiven you
2. i kissed you to try and get
   over number one i stole your first kiss
   you said i was your first love too
   i didn't love you sometimes i think
   about your face when i told you the truth
   i have never stopped being sorry
1. when you came back i thought you'd
   changed you promised things were
   different i believed you because
   i had never stopped loving you and
   things were great until i realized you'd
   never stopped loving her either
3. you were sad and i thought i could
   save you but you can't just kiss
   depression away i will always regret
   giving up on you so soon but i am
   too selfish for someone as pure as you
   you deserve the best in the world and
   i thank you for finally forgiving me
4. i will always smile when i think of you
   there was nothing wrong with us you
   just can't fix something that was built
   already broken down i truly believe that
   you've always belonged with her
   i was just a road stop on the way
5. i thought you were the end i meant
   every promise i ever made to you
   but instead of talking to me you were
   making out with girls you didn't care
   about and that's when you started to
   slowly break my heart
6. i wanted to show number five i could

kiss my friends for fun too i didn't mean
to fall in love with you i'm sorry i made you
want to kill yourself when i ended it but i
hope you've grown up because threatening
suicide won't make me love you again
5. i guess i didn't realize how much you loved
me until you almost lost me to number six
but we will never find someone who loves us
as much as we love each other we are
soulmates and you kissed another girl
it doesn't matter you're my soulmate right
7. you were the kindest person i'd ever
met you bought me gifts and told me
i was pretty but you didn't like how
i would shout my opinions and when i
refused to change you left i learned that night
that no boy is worth changing who you are
5. you had me wrapped around your finger
and my heart locked in a cage you would stab
it whenever i'd try to pull away so while
you were kissing someone else i broke in
and took it back after all those months
i finally took it back
8. you've loved me for a long time and i'm
sorry it took me so long to figure it out
but i'm here now and i don't plan on leaving
you are mine and i am yours forever and
always i will love you for forever and always
i promise i promise i promise
5. i finally get why you'd kiss other girls and
not worry about losing me i now know what
it's like to have someone love you so much
you could do anything and they would stay
the difference is that i wouldn't ever act on it
i don't want to break him like you did me
5. i'm sorry i'm sorry i'm sorry i'm sorry i'm
sorry i'm sorry i'm sorry i'm sorry i'm sorry
i'm sorry i'm sorry i'm sorry i'm sorry i'm sorry
i'm sorry i'm sorry i'm sorry i'm sorry i'm sorry

i'm sorry i'm sorry i'm sorry i'm sorry i'm sorry
and i shouldn't be

5. do you realize now how much you meant to
    me how i had counted on us if you called for
    help i would still come to you if you needed a
    friend i would be there in a strange way you
    are still mine and i am still yours but we were
    never meant to be forever and always

in the end i have to save myself

he says that he loves me
because he has to.
not because he wants to,
or needs to,
but because he has to.

as if i am a burden for him
that he can't leave out of fear
that i will not be able to carry myself--
as if i am dependent on him and
his half-hearted attempts to
make me feel happy.

he says:
but you need me, i cannot leave you.
i say:
i can learn not to need you,
for what is a bigger waste of time
than holding the hand of someone
who is a ghost of the love they used
to give you?

i tell him this:
for him to not love me and leave
would break my bones
and leave me breathless,
but for him to not love me and stay
would crumble me to dust
and render me unable to breathe
ever again.

i didn't think this needed an explanation

but i'm going to explain it
anyway

i write about love
because it is
what i know
i write about pain
because it is
what i've felt
i write about abuse
because it is
what i've been through
i write about politics
because it is
what i care about

i write about
what i have
experienced
i write about
what makes me
quake with anger
heave with sadness
smile with joy

i will never write
for anybody
but myself

i will never write
something that
i don't mean

i know my art
will not reach everybody
and i have never
expected it to

but i expect—
no
i *demand*—
respect as an artist
because that
is what
i deserve

bias

when i am talking
to a boy and he finds out
that i write poetry,
the first thing he asks is,

"will you ever write about me?"

i tell him honestly,
"hopefully, i won't."

and he asks,
"why?"

it's my answer that
always catches them.

"because,
if i end up writing about you,
it means that all the promises
you made me
ended up being broken
and maybe you're somebody
i shouldn't have spent so much
time on
if all you were going to do
in the end is
break my heart."

if they're smart,
they call me on it.
tell me that every
relationship is worth it
because you always have
something to learn.
in the end,
these are the boys
i write about most.

but if they love me,
they stay quiet.
because the thought
of them breaking my heart
is enough to suck the
words from their tongues.

these are the boys
i don't write about.
not because they aren't there,
but because i cast the
fatal blow.

and even now,
i have never been good
at saying sorry.

oceans, the future

i watch the brown waves
stumble against the shore.
the water sloshes against
my shins, hot and oily.

plastic bags wrap around
my ankles
like seaweed,
bottle caps crunch
under my toes:
the new seashell.

i walk along the
glass-bedded sand
and trace my feet
through soda tabs.

a turtle limps by,
its neck strangled
by a six-pack ring.

i am so thrilled
to see an animal,
i don't even notice
it can barely breathe.

it's not a good time to talk about it

i cradle a 5-year old's body in my arms
watch the blood trickle from his chest
wonder if this will ever be okay to talk about
if we will ever be able to stomach it enough
to talk about the murder of twenty elementary schoolers

so the news cycle continues and they point fingers
at what is to blame— if it's the guns or the mental health
or the violent video games
and they point fingers so much that they forget
to actually do something about it

so the years pass and i hold the hands of
thousands with red bubbling at their lips
and i listen to the politicians saying now isn't
a good time to talk about it
maybe they want to wait for
the parents to stop screaming
the lovers to stop hurting
the friends to stop crying

but it won't stop
because the violence won't stop
and i touch the cheek of a dead kindergartener
wonder if maybe it's not that we can't stomach it
it's that we can and we do every single day
and that's why twenty dead children weren't enough
to make us change.

the saddest thing

in the weeks after,
i traced my fingers along
the cracks in the porcelain
in my heart and i could
still feel the imprint
where your hands
used to rest.

there are chips missing,
exposing the bleeding red
beneath, and i know
that those pieces
rest in your pocket.

of course,
you had to leave
with some sort of
piece of me.

i'm not angry
that you took
a part of my heart.

i'm just sad,
because even though
you have it,
it won't make us
any less of strangers.

ivory
i wonder if they notice

how i touch piano keys
like they can breathe

succubus

i'm still waiting
for the bite marks
to heal.

a misconstrued metaphor

people say that the way you know
how loved a book is
is by how worn the pages are.
how creased the spine is.
how wrinkled the corners are
from bending them.

i want to think that
you took this idea
to heart when it came
to how you treated me.
maybe you thought
the more broken and bent
i was the more loved i would look.

but i am not a book.
you cannot pick me up
just to put me down again.
i am not something to be skimmed.
read all of me, or don't read any at all.

i'm not demanding
you take forever
to finish me.
i won't even mind
if you don't enjoy me.

i'm just asking that
you treat me with care,
and walk away having learned
something new.

honest texts to my ex i'm too scared to send

you can't keep resurfacing like a rotted fish in the ocean on a hot day. it makes me sick, every time.

i don't care if you dreamt about me. please don't let me know that i still haunt you at night. it'll make me think there's still something here.

sometimes i'm afraid i might still be in love with you. out of everything, that's what i'm most scared of.

i want you to know that i miss the way you made me laugh. can we have that again someday?

you still make me cry, you fuck

you always tell me you're still not okay but what about me? what makes you think i'm okay? i had my heart broken too, remember?

nothing felt as easy at the beginning as you did. but nothing was as impossible in the end as you were.

i'm sorry. i've always been sorry.

i don't think i'm ever going to love somebody like i loved you, but i'm okay with that. i don't want to feel this type of pain ever again.

one day, you're going to look back on me and smile. you'll have to.

we can't dwell on this forever.

write about something other than love
that is what they tell me
they say
to write about something
more challenging than love

like coming to terms
with your abusive relationship
isn't challenging

like learning to stop
loving someone who
once gave you everything
isn't a battle

like figuring out
how to use art as
a catharsis instead of
not sleeping
not eating
not breathing
isn't a hard thing to do

so this is me saying
i will write about whatever
makes me scream
makes me cry
makes me laugh
makes me smile

and if that's love
or a lack thereof
then so be it

i didn't bleed
just so you could say
my blood isn't
red enough
for you

and until we meet again

i stand here at the precipice.
i do not want to be one who looks back at high school
as if they were the best times of my life.
the best, for me, has yet to come.
but the best times of my life so far have often happened within
the white-bricked walls of your classroom.

sicut erat--
since the beginning.
since the beginning of music there have been people like you,
people who love and cherish every note, every syllable.
i have always wanted to be one of the masters,
and these last four years i have been learning from the best.

i stand here at the precipice.
the world awaits me.
the music of my future is calling.
i look back upon the music of my past,
and you.

go, you say. *go and make the best
of this messed up world.*

thank you, i reply.
*thank you for reminding me i have a voice
on the days where i could barely make a sound.*

writer's block

and i wish i could write
about you,
because i want to tell
the world
how beautiful you are
to me.

but i can't,
and as you press
your lips into my
collarbone,
i think,

maybe this is a good thing.
maybe this is just
for us.

gravedigger

here lie all the sentences cut short by my indecisiveness
all the periods stapled on after words that weren't meant
to be the finish

i run my hands through frostbitten soil
and scrape my palms on headstones
where the bloodiest poems of mine are buried—
funny how each one is engraved with your name

and i will not apologize for writing about you
just like you will never apologize for making me
not because you aren't sorry
but because you don't realize that it's your fault

i didn't ask to be a poet
although it is my fault that i've let it ruin my life
i wish i could stifle the urge to bleed onto pages
i wish i didn't have to bury every sweet song
you had ever whispered in my ear

is this a love poem or an apology letter?
i can't tell the difference between them anymore—
mostly because i love you, but i'm sorry for it.

an excerpt (#4)

it was there the second i stepped into the room: the tension. it soaked the air, so thick i could have sworn i would have been able to press my fingers into it had i tried. it didn't take long for me to figure out why—although i did see it coming.

i knew he would be here.

i found it cruel, cruel of whoever, or whatever, was in charge of fate, to bring us together again. not here. this, of all places, was the most haunted. when our eyes met, i knew he was thinking the same thing.

it took all i had to walk towards him, and it felt like i was stepping on glass shards the entire time. with every inch, another memory blasted itself into my mind. i could see the ghosts of us, i could feel his touches, and even now, they made my heart stop. which, more than anything, was what made it so terrifying.

and then, i was standing in front of him. he looked the same; a little sadder, maybe, but i suppose i was wearing the same broken expression.

he spoke first, just like he always did. "hi."

the single syllable jarred me. i let his voice wash over me like melted gold-- it was always one of my favorite things about him. after a few seconds, i managed to reply. "hi. i didn't expect to see you here." a lie, of course, and he knew it.

but he chose to ignore it. "how have you been?"

"good," i told him, and it was the truth: i had been good, great, even, but being here, with him, was starting to pick away at my progress. i could feel it decaying, and it had only been a few minutes. "what about you?"

 "better, i've been better," he answered, and then he gestured to the seat next to him. "would you like to sit?"

no. but i did, and the fight within me died quickly as i registered just how close we were. closer than we had been in months. almost as close as we had been before. my heart pounded.

he could tell i was a disaster; i had always been bad at hiding my emotions. but i knew him, almost better than i knew myself, and i could see him cracking. every glance i cast towards him sent another fragment falling to the ground. he was already in pieces—my handiwork, of course.

finally, he cut through the fragile silence. "i just, um... i guess i wasn't as prepared for, for... this," he said, slowly, as if he were handpicking every individual letter.

"yeah," i agreed, as carefully as him, "it's... it's a lot harder, than i, i thought it would be."

"does that mean that—" he stopped himself. i wanted to press him, tell him to finish it, but when i looked at him, his eyes finished it for me.

the hope.

does that mean that you still love me? he was asking. *does that mean we still have a chance?*

"no." the word tasted like acid on my tongue, and i almost choked it out, "it just means it still hurts."
"i'm sorry," he whispered, and i hated it. hated to see him like this: so quiet and cracked. hated to see us like this: the exact opposite of what we were. we had become what we promised we never would: strangers.

 "i know you are. and i—i'm trying to forgive you, i am. but it's hard. and this, this is hard." the truth. it always seemed to come out so easily around him. i'd never understood it. "i want us to be able to be friends," i confessed, "like we were before. because i was your friend first. and i loved that." almost as much as i loved you, i finished in my head.

he ran a hand through his hair. "i don't—i don't know. i don't think i'm okay yet. everything hurts still, you know? and there are days where i'm fine but then something reminds me of you or you show up in a dream and everything just hits me like a brick, that i had you, and now i don't, and i caused it—" he was rambling, and he knew it, but it didn't stop him, "i mean, even this, this is killing me right now," his voice shook, "and i don't know when i'm going to be able to look at you and—and not love you."

i said nothing, because there was nothing to be said. i knew all of this. he'd told me a thousand times; begged for me to come back, and each time, i said no. i had to. for myself, and for him. we were breaking each other.

"i just wish... i just wish i could do it all over again." his hand grazed mine, and i flinched. across the room, the ghosts of us sat together, fingers intertwined, heads huddled close together in a tender conversation. they had no idea of what was to come. i remembered how sweet it all was, and the taste seemed to wash over my mouth like syrup.

he touched my hand again, and i jolted away from the past. it was over, and i couldn't do anything to change it.
but i could do something now.

his fingers brushed against mine, and i faced a dilemma.

i could push him off and walk away. close this door for good. i couldn't let it stay as it was: left slightly ajar, inviting him inside, but never completely. he always had to push a little. but i could also take the jump. i could reach out and take his hand, and we could try again. i could see it in front of me. i knew we loved each other. and sitting in the place where it all began, remembering how gentle and soft it had been, i wanted to believe that we could resurrect it. that we could learn from our mistakes, and we could make it.

but i also remembered what tore us apart. his arrogance, and my paranoia. his selfishness, and my tendency to go the self-preservation route. his secrets, and my hypocrisy. the lack of communication, and the distance. of course, always the distance.

i looked down at his hand, and up into his eyes.

"take it," he pleaded, his blue eyes glistening, "please. we can do it."

and i did. i let my fingers intertwine with his and for a second a warmth washed over me. i looked around, and i saw the ghosts around us. us, kissing in the corner. us, cuddled on a bench. us, happy, unbroken. and for a moment, i couldn't differentiate between my memories and the present.

which was the problem.

i pulled my hand back, ignoring the cold, sick feeling puddling in my chest. he looked shattered. "why?"

"because," i said, "because when we're here, we're haunted by what we were. all we see in this place is the beginning of us, the part of us that wasn't torn or broken or poisoned. and we can't go back to that. we just—can't. you've hurt me too many times. lied to me, made me cry. and i've hurt you, made empty promises and then walked them back, left you behind while i moved on. we can't get this," and i gestured to our past, "back. it's impossible. we're broken. and we need to, we need to be with people who can fix us. and that isn't what we are for each other. that's just... that's just the way it is." i stood. "i'm sorry, i am. but we can't keep falling into this trap. you're not moving on because you keep thinking there's a chance for us. but there isn't. and i hope that hearing it from me helps you break away from this, whatever it is."

"but, i love you," he murmured, looking down at his hands. they were speckled with tears. "isn't that enough?"

"no. not anymore." i felt tears gathering in my eyes. it hurt to say it. it hurt so, so much. but i had to. "i'm so sorry. but you'll be okay. i know you'll be okay. i have to do this. it's the only way."

"only way for you," he snapped, and although it was soft, it was laced with anger.

"no. it's the only way for you." i turned. "you may not see it right now, but one day, you'll thank me for this. i couldn't let myself keep breaking you." and then i was gone, walking swiftly out the door.

as i left, the ghosts of us swirled around me, and i took one last look over my shoulder. he had left. in his place, was the apparitions of two broken lovers; he reaches for her hand, and she walks away with the shattered determination of someone who was fighting not to turn around.

"thank you," i breathed, to nobody but the air.

"thank you for showing me how to save myself."

excerpt from the story of us

"i'm giving up on you," she declared, ignoring the way her voice shook and her stomach plummeted as she said it. "i'm giving up on you, not because i want to, but because i have to. for both of us. you don't love me anymore, and i know this now. i've been holding out hope that maybe there was something there, something lingering, but i've figured it all out."

she held his gaze as best she could, looking past the pain in his eyes, the protest blooming on his lips. "when we met, we didn't know what would happen," she continued, "we didn't know the people we'd meet or the things that would happen. we had no clue. we tried to predict it by betting on our futures being each other, but you can't gamble with fate. fate will always win. i put, i put my whole heart into you–us, and look how that turned out," with that, she laughed, all dry and broken. "but none of that matters now. you chose otherwise. and i did, too. i'm not free of blame, here."

he tried to speak, reach out to her, but she pushed his hand away, quieting him. "i fell in love with him because i thought… i thought we weren't an option anymore. because you were always gone, gone when i wanted you and gone when i needed you. i tried so hard to keep us alive. i ignored the fact that the writing on the wall was no longer just writing; it was carved into the plaster. i blocked out what my friends said, because they didn't know us, they didn't know you. but what they did know was that with every day that passed, i cracked more and more. they could see it on my face, in my actions, in the way i talked about you. fuck, they realized you were breaking me long before i did."

"i'm sorry," he whimpered, "i'm so sorry, just please–"

"no," she whispered, and her eyes clouded with tears, "don't you see? i can't. you can't take back what you did to me. i needed you, you fuck. more than anybody else, i needed you. and you weren't there. she wasn't just a friend, and it wasn't just a kiss, and you knew it too. but you lied and dragged me along because you knew i was so hurt i wouldn't have the strength to leave."

she smiled, suddenly, "but he had the strength. and he saved me, and he opened my eyes. to the reality of what we were. he gave me everything i ever wanted from you– and i never asked for much. and more. he gave me so much more, things i never dreamed of with you. so you can't blame me for falling in love with him. you can't blame me for getting tired."

"but you promised–"

"i know what i promised, and i tried to keep it. i really, really did. you were the one that fell through. you were the one that stopped replying. you were the one that left my messages ignored. you were the one that wasn't there to congratulate me on my accomplishments, or comfort me on my failures." she paused, and although her voice trembled, she felt stronger now before him than she ever had before. "but me? i kept the conversations going. i asked you how your day was. i was your biggest fan and the best friend you could have ever fucking had, even after all the shit you threw at me. but none of that seemed to matter to you, so i finally got it. i finally understood what the lack of replies meant."

"and what," he murmured, "did it mean?"

"it meant," she said simply, "that it's time to give up on you. i don't think you really want me around anymore, now that i'm not in love with you. i'm not a pretty girl you can show off to boost your ego. i never was. i was more than that, or at least i was supposed to be. i deserved more. and i got it. after all this time, i got it. and just because that hurts your fucking feelings," she pointed her finger at his face, her eyes sparked with anger, "doesn't meant i'm going to throw it all away. so i'm giving up on you, finally. i'm sorry that i wasn't worth your time until i didn't want it anymore."

autopsy

sometimes, i get into ruts where i relive
all my relationships
and i dissect them
as though they were frogs
in anatomy class.

i peel back the surface
as though it were a layer of skin
and then i pick my way
through the insides of each one
and i try to make myself
understand again where it went wrong.
what it was that made the heart stop beating.
as if understanding why it died
would resurrect it
so i could maybe give
a couple another chance.

i especially spend a lot
of time digging through
the corpse of us.
each time, it is
more rotted than the last.

and as the organs shrivel
and the bones begin to crumble
i find out more about us.
i pull out lies from between the ribs
and the things we left unsaid from its stomach.
in its heart, i discover that it was
broken long before it stopped beating.

at some point,
i will have torn our remains
apart.
much like we did
to each other.

out of habit

i tore stars from my veins for you
spit up my dreams into your outstretched hand
wiped the corner of my mouth and smiled through the burning in
my throat.
you tapped the lock on my chest
and i should have known then that nothing would ever be
enough for you.
but i handed you the key because for once i was determined
to not let the voices in my head get the better of me.

i told myself that i had to stop ripping my relationships apart at
the seams
so i let you rip me apart instead.
in the end i don't think my love was unrequited
but i do think it was unappreciated.
i want to think that you had no idea what you were doing
but i know you saw me the day after
and i also know that you never apologized.

love is cynical and honest
i tell myself that it only wants what's best for me
yet i keep finding myself bearing my back
handing them the knife
closing my eyes
looking the other way.
trying to convince myself that the gashes on my skin came from
a stranger
and not the person i slept next to.

i'm starting to wonder if maybe love is trying to teach me a
lesson
and i have just refused to learn it.

among the gray

i watch our story on rewind
in black and white.

sometimes i wish i could
see the blue of your irises
but i don't think i'll ever be able
to picture us in color again.

i don't love you anymore,
i know better than that now,

but i still find myself writing about you
late at night when i forget how to breathe
and it's like,

how do i learn to breathe again
without it being because of you?

i traded a kind love for a powerful love,
and you gave me it--

i still find traces of you in every damn thing,
the backseat of a car and the booth of a restaurant,
i guess in a way we're lasting like we said we would,
and you know,

i think about you on friday nights
when my friends are out drinking and i'm sitting at home
writing this stupid fucking book about you
because for some reason i can still trace the shape of your mouth
with my finger in the mirror, even now,

and i don't think i love you anymore
because it's not that i miss you,
it's not that i want you back,
it's just that i still have to justify
why i'm always looking for
skeletons in their closet, i still leave the door open because

i don't want to make their awaited exit any more painful,

and the thing is,
the reason why i can't stop writing about you,
is that despite the cracks in my cheeks
and the way my hands shake when i touch his chest,
how i can't seem to stop looking over my shoulder,

i still don't regret a single fucking thing.

the train is coming
so i kiss you
goodbye at the
station

some things
are not meant to last

forever

i leave you
because i
have to

i leave you
like i was
always meant
to go.

a double-edged sword

and the hot, heavy truth
of it is that i can write about
all you did to me
as much as i want,
but it doesn't change the fact that
i hurt you
too.

reincarnate

i think in our previous lives, we've always been in love with each other, estranged and held apart by a thin thread.

you were the king's son and i was a peasant girl.
i was an aristocrat and you worked in the stables.
i was in love with somebody else.
you were in love with somebody else.

the first time we met, the world must have stopped in its tracks. because when i first saw you in this lifetime, i felt everything freeze.

we have always loved each other from afar, each lifetime drawing us closer and closer.

the first time, you accepted a flower from me when you were riding through my village. you rode through it often, and one time you stopped, got down from your carriage and spoke to me. but you were soon married to a princess, just like all princes were.

the second time, you helped me learn how to ride and take care of my horse. sometimes our hands would brush when we groomed him together. you were my confidant. my friend. we never once told each other what we really felt.

the third time, you were my neighbor, my best friend, and one night you kissed me during a game of hide and seek. "i love you," you'd said to me, and for a second i loved you too. but a few weeks later i started dating somebody else. that summer, you moved away. in that lifetime, i broke your heart.

the fourth time, we had each other, for a while. our families vacationed by the same lake. you didn't tell me you had girlfriend until you had seen everything i had to offer you. you watched me cry in front of you. your family left the next day. in that lifetime, you broke mine.

our souls knew each other before we did. they found each other from across the room and pulled us together. "it's you," they said to one another, "i'm so glad it's you. maybe we can get it right this time." and then it began, again.

this time, we could have made it if we had had the strength. the courage. but i was afraid and your heart wasn't there. eventually, mine wandered too. we drifted, our souls still reaching out for each other even though our hands no longer were.

but this time, we knew.
this time, we told each other.
this time, we fought.

in this lifetime, there wasn't an issue of who broke who.
in this lifetime, we merely broke each other.

i know it's heartbreaking to think we never got a real chance. your sobs ring as loud in my ears now as they did the day we shattered, and they haunt me.

our time in this life together is over. we lost this round. but each lifetime, we inch closer and closer.

and in my heart, i hope.
my soul, it longs for you still.

it has picked itself out of the rubble of yet another failure and pieced itself back together.

my soul, it knows.

"i will find you again," it whispers into the cosmos,
"there are many lifetimes to come."

from across the world, your soul returns,
"we will get our chance yet."

in between the lines

in response to the message i received last december from my abusive ex-boyfriend asking me why i keep writing about him even though i'm dating somebody else:

wouldn't you like to know?

i know you still think you're the innocent one, that you don't deserve to have all the lies you told split open on the operating table, all the moments between us dissected like cadavers.

as if you didn't leave me with crippling paranoia. the inability to trust somebody when they say they care about me. a debilitating fear of abandonment.

you said that it was inappropriate of me, that i was beating a dead horse.

you even had the audacity to tell me it hurt you. all the poems. all the prose pieces. the pain it put you through, to see me ripping through our relationship like canines ripping into flesh.

so maybe i'm writing this because i'm tired of choking on your arrogance. i'm finished with letting you think you got away with something, like i'm just fragile, easily cracked, hard to repair.

but i'll tell you why i haven't stopped writing about you.

because i can't.

i want to, but i haven't figured out how to stop when i see you around every corner.

because every time i think about the stars i think about your hands, and every time i find myself in the backseat of a car i can feel it closing in on me like your mouth.

because i'm afraid i won't be able to love him as much as i can.

do you know how that feels? to be afraid to love somebody?
i look at him and i see somebody who is softer than me.

because he fits into my side like a jigsaw piece but sometimes
his voice lilts and it sounds like yours for a heartbeat and in that
single second i forget you aren't here anymore.

because sometimes i forget you aren't here anymore.

i didn't ask to be stuck to you. i didn't want to still be bleeding a
year later. but you have to ask yourself how deep this wound
must be if i'm still not healed. you have to start looking at
yourself. maybe you really were the monster. maybe you are.

but you won't. and that's why i'm still writing about you.
because you can't see it. you can't even fathom the thought that i
wasn't just made this way. it wasn't somebody else who left
gashes across my throat. it was you. and you can't see it. or you
won't. i'm not sure which one it is anymore.

i keep writing because you never said sorry.

you will never understand, and you will never apologize. i don't
know if you weren't paying attention when i was telling you to
stop or if you heard it and just didn't care. now i'm not even sure
if that matters anymore, you caring or not. it never felt like it.

i keep writing because i don't know how to feel about us now.
because you were so important and i don't even know what to
call you.

because i can't tell if you were a forest fire or a hurricane, but
either way you ravaged me.

because when you left you did not leave quietly, you left on a
war path, smashing in the windowpanes and ripping out the
ceiling lights,
because you left reminders: your spit splattered across the walls;
your bloodied fingerprints smeared on the door frame,

because i am still too weak to be able to wash them away, because i will probably always be too weak.

that is what you did to me.

for a long time, there wasn't anything left to build from.

i was bent beams and shattered glass with dusty kneecaps and rusted elbows, sitting out on the curb waiting for the garbage truck to come.

i didn't know how to look in the mirror anymore without being afraid i would see you lurking over my shoulder.

eventually, i learned how to breathe again. i began to wipe the dirt from my cheeks and brush the blood from my mouth. i learned to stand on my own without you grasping my arm. i trained myself to smile; a different grin, one you wouldn't recognize. i taught myself how to unlove you.

so here i am, a year later.

the soft boy clicks into my hip and i am still writing about you. you want to know if i'm still in love with you, if that's why the poems never stop.
it's not because i love you, or because i care at all.

it's because there's a long white scar on my chest from your claws.
because he touches it sometimes and that's the one part of my body where we don't fit like puzzle pieces, where we don't fit at all.
because that's the one part that's still yours.

i will write as many words as it takes to color it in.

for you
it gets better
than this.

the hurt.
the ache.

i know it seems
like you're going
to be stuck in this pit
forever,

but it gets better.

this wound will
heal no matter how
long it takes.

flashback

i'm very scared of having my heart broken again. more than anything in my future, i am most scared of that, because i can control everything else. i can work hard and practice and be strong and everything i want will fall into place. but i can't stop him from falling out of love with me. i can't make him hold on to me longer than he wants to. i remember the last time somebody i loved told me they'd stopped loving me. i was 13. i remember the feeling in my chest: the rotting, gaping feeling, even now, whenever i think of their name. i barely ate for weeks. the crying was almost constant. my only salvation was writing, and to this day it's the only thing that saves me from falling back into that when something starts to fall apart. i was so careful to make sure that the last person who broke my heart did it slowly, in doses, so i had time to heal each crack before the next one came. so when he left, i wasn't shattered, i was worn out. i was bruised. but i wasn't up at three am dry heaving into a toilet. i wasn't shaking in the shower with the water so hot my skin was bright red. i breathed. i cried. and i continued on. but with him, with him i am so scared. because i don't see an end. i don't see a gradual crumbling into ruin. the end for us is either nonexistent or earth-shattering, a lightning strike, a tornado, sudden and deadly. i haven't felt that way since i was 13. in so many ways, he makes me feel young. but this is one way that i don't want him to.

novel

i like to take my inspiration from things around me, and i have to admit that you are the source of almost all my poetry now. the ink that drips from my fingertips is only because you have kissed them, and i don't understand how one person can take so much of me, and how i am willing to just let them. i write paragraphs on the shape of your lips and whole stories on just how you got the scar on your thigh. i love details, i love to describe and elaborate, so i write stanzas just on how it felt to hold your hand for the first time, and they say this is silly love, this is foolish love, but i have never felt more serious about something. you are the one thing that keeps me walking on the days where i can barely stand. i do not know what is to come, but i do know that no matter what, years from now, i will pull our book from the shelf, blow the dust off the cover, and lose myself in you once more.

i'll have a caramel macchiato // the couple in the corner of the coffee shop

they have a table,
and it's theirs but also not theirs,
because you can't really own a table
in a coffee shop but also you don't really
see anybody else sitting there but them.

and what i mean by that is,
even when they're not there, they're there,
because that's their table, in their corner,
where he smiles at her for no reason at all
other than the light hit her cheekbones just right,
or maybe he just wants to smile at her because
they're in that kind of love where you just smile,
all the time.
and she stares at him when he isn't looking,
and anybody could see that he just takes her breath away
because when she watches him, time seems to freeze
until he looks up and catches her,
and then he just smiles at her and her eyelids flutter
like freshly blossomed butterfly wings
and they laugh like it's some sort of secret,
this game that they have where he smiles
and she stares and then they both smile together,
like nobody else could even begin to understand.

she orders a caramel macchiato
because she likes sweet things
and he orders a cappuccino
because he doesn't sleep enough.
i didn't think those drinks were
supposed to go together until
i saw the two of them sipping
in the corner.
they don't speak much.
they don't add to the white noise
of conversation, and you find yourself

watching them because you don't need
to hear them to know.

she reads poetry
and he works on his laptop
but sometimes, she will reach out
and show him a line she likes,
but sometimes, he will tap the top of the page
she's reading and have her listen to a song
he's working on,
but sometimes, they will just look up
and he will reach out and grab her hand
and tell her he loves her, or that she looks especially
beautiful today, or she will compliment his eyes,
or remind him of how happy he makes her,
and they don't do it because there's a need
for reassurance, they just do it because they want to.
because the words feel good wrapped around them.

when she leaves, she kisses him.
it's short like a heartbeat but it's like
she needs it to get through her day.
like the stain of his lips will make
her lecture less painful.

you wonder if she tastes like starlight.
you wonder how ocean water would taste
from the hollow of her collarbone.
he looks like he knows all of it and then some.

you order a caramel macchiato and wonder if
one day you'll get a sip of something like that.

2018

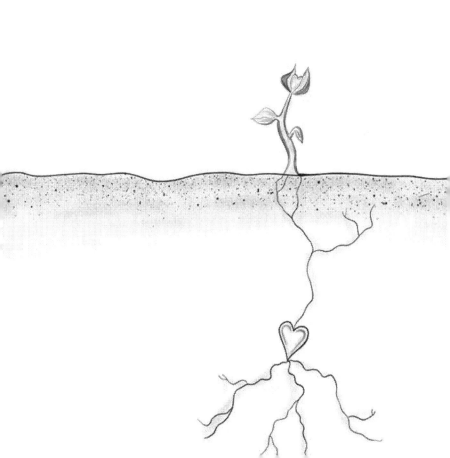

apology

i want to be sorry
for the rusty nail
metaphors
and the sloppy
analogies.

i want to regret
all the poetry
that split us open
like a gaping wound.

i want to feel bad
for writing about you.
i want to feel bad
for letting everybody
witness the aftermath
of you, of us.

but i can't be sorry.

i am not sorry
for doing what
i had to do.

i am not sorry
for fixing the damage
you inflicted upon me.

i am not sorry
for writing about you.

i am just sorry
that i had to.

apology, part 2

you will never understand
what you did
and for that,
i am sorry.

but it is no longer
my job
to tell you.

switch

at some point,
i stopped romanticizing
our story.

i stopped writing off
my pain as part
of the fairytale.

i put down all the blame
you'd laid on me
and realized that
it was never
my
fault.

haunting

i see you in the mirror sometimes,
in my own reflection.

you said,
"i will be part of you.
i will always be part of you."

since when did that change
from a fond memory
to my own personal
ghost?

the reason why
my mother tells me
i was always too foolish,
that i fall for people too quick
and too hard.

she says she hates to see
me hurting again and again.

she asks me if this is worth it.

and i show her the poetry.

xanthophyll

you made me hate
the changing of the seasons.
the crumbling of what was.

i was so afraid of you leaving
i didn't realize there was
a chance for something
after you.

when i'm old
i wonder if i will
look back upon
all the ones who
gave me my firsts.

if i will glance over
my shoulder at
the hands still reaching
for me,
the lips still parted
in the shape of my name.

him, with the tongue
scraping at the ground
where i stepped.
him, with the fists
of daffodils and
violet smile.
him, with too much.
him, still standing there.

him, waiting.
and me,
just going.

landmine

i used to be one of those people that didn't really understand triggers and how the simplest of things could send you tumbling down a rabbit hole back into that memory. i never understood how something like a word or making breakfast or the way somebody says a sentence could cause your stomach to heave and your mouth to go dry and your fists to clench so tightly that you think your palms are bleeding. i never understood any of that. i never got how somebody's mind could be wired to such give such tiny, irrelevant things such big meanings, how a syllable could become the equivalent to a landmine, how a gesture could become the same thing as a trip wire.

and then you happened. and i got it. i got it too well. i understood because then suddenly, somebody reaching over to rub my back would make me go still. too still. and for a few seconds, i wouldn't be able to move because it wasn't my friend, it was you. suddenly, somebody is singing a song you used to sing and i have to leave the room because i can feel my heart trying to claw its way out of my throat. it took me over a year to let somebody call me angel again because that was what you called me and every time i thought i was ready to be over all the stupid minuscule bullshit parts of us i just wasn't. i'm still just not. you commented on one of my photos a few months back and it ruined my entire day. i could not let it go. i can't let it go.

and maybe this isn't what having a trigger is like, but it sure feels like there are landmines peppered everywhere i go and tripwires all around me for other people to get tangled up in so they can watch me run, or cry, or do absolutely nothing at all.

maybe this is the remnants of the heartbreak i never realized was happening until it was too late to fix it. maybe it's just that, and maybe i'm not as fucked up as i think i am.
but it feels like i stepped off one battlefield just to get caught up in another. it feels like you're not gone no matter how much i wish you were, but i can't bring myself to block you because that would mean you're definitely gone, and i don't think i want that, yet. or at all.

is this what abuse does to people? this back and forth, this tiptoeing around? is this what an aftermath is like? because i want to go back to not knowing how this feels. i want to go back to not getting it and not understanding how small things could rip you to shreds within seconds. i'm so tired of being scared to walk around. i just want the mines and wires to disappear. i just want to stop being afraid of being detonated.

i should've seen it coming

he says
well you see, i've been talking to another girl
it's no big deal but just thought you should know

i say
yeah that's okay, you know i like this one guy too
and he makes my heart pound

he says
you still love me right?

i say
of course i do
it's all just fun anyway right
right

he says
yeah yeah just for fun
you know i wouldn't leave you

they say
that seems pretty fucked up
maybe you should cut it off

i say
haha, that's funny, actually it's just fine
it's an agreement, we've got it all worked out

they say
then why do you keep writing sad shit
about the one you love not treating you right

i say
because i'm sad with an overactive imagination
that's unrelated though

they say
bullshit

i say
no it's fine, trust me, he loves me
he wouldn't dare

he says
i kissed her

i say
okay
do you still love me

he says
well don't you have that other guy
the one you like a lot

i say
do you still love me

he says
you should go out with that guy more
i think it'd be good for you

they say
fucking run

i say
i can't, don't you get it
i just can't

he says
i just think it would be good for you

i say
do you still love me

he says
well if i'm being honest
i'm not sure anymore

they say
we told you so

i say
are you fucking kidding me

the broken girls

we do not exist
for your poetry

we can tell our stories
ourselves

stop making us your muse
when we didn't ask
to be

users

some people do nothing but
take
take
take

they leave licking their lips
full of you

and you stay
trying to refill yourself
in case another one
comes along

you have never wanted
to be a disappointment.

i have taken
jab after jab
wound after wound
pain after so much pain
from you.

you would think at some point
i would have learned my lesson.

and yet i wrap the wounds
each time.

apologizing for bleeding.
still.

untitled

"i think you're really beautiful."
"must be nice."
"what does that mean?"
"must be nice to not hate what you see, is what i mean."

~

"when was the last time somebody hurt you?"
"i don't get hurt. i just hurt."
"what?"
"this is your warning."

~

"have you ever fallen in love?"
"i wouldn't know."
"but..."
"but what?"

~

"i keep trying to tell you how i feel but you aren't listening—"
"i never asked for this. you."
"well, you got me. i'm here."
"i know."

~

"i love you."
"i'm sorry."

~

"i love you."
"stop saying it."

~

"i have to let you go. for my sake. you're hurting me."

"i've been telling you that since the beginning."
"i know. i should've listened."

~

"..."
"i'm sorry. i told you."

~

"..."
"i miss you, sometimes.

~

"..."
"i love you."

~

"i'm sorry."
"..."

reincarnate, part 2

i wrote once that he was my soulmate,
but we kept getting it wrong.

each lifetime would bring us a step closer,
but we would always find ourselves ripped apart.

now i think that we fell apart
so that i could fall into you.

we never got it right because
we weren't supposed to.

you say that it feels as if you've known me
for your whole life.

i think we have known each other for lifetimes.

we have a love story of centuries,
each recycling only building upon what has already

been created.

a poet's growth

for as long as i have been writing,
i have been afraid
of being called
cliché,
unoriginal,
of being accused
of fitting into a mold
of some stereotype.

but over time,
i have learned that
my heart
is unlike anybody else's.
it bears scars
nobody else could have.
my experiences
are my own.
my story
is mine to tell.

and my poetry?

it is my heart,
slashed open,
bleeding across these pages.

it would be a disservice
to myself if my words
were anything
but honest.

what i have learned (and what you must learn too)

every story
has a lesson.

every poem
has a purpose.

if you are writing,
there is a reason.

do not ignore
the pain boiling
inside of you.

if the pen calls,
go to it.

i only wish
i had gone
to it
sooner.

girls

girls like her may always look put together, well-trimmed and polished.
girls like her may always look like they stepped straight out of their packaging.

girls like her might make you feel venomous.
girls like her might make you green with envy and red with rage.
girls like her may have everything they want, and everything you want, too.
girls like her may make you forget that despite what you tell yourself,

girls like her have bad days and bad pasts just like the rest of us.
girls like her come from poor families. girls like her have abusive partners.
girls like her are stuffed full of regrets and secrets and riddled with scars.

girls like her are no different from girls like you.
girls like her may look at girls like you and want to switch places.
girls like her might want to see a girl like you in the mirror.

girls like her can be unhappy.
girls like her may not want to be part of girls like her.
girls like her do not deserve unjustified hatred.

girls like you are just as beautiful.
girls like you have to remember that.
and girls like you have to learn that

girls like her and girls like you are just girls.
girls are beautiful.
girls are exquisite.
girls do not need to compete with each other for first place.
there is no first place. there is no trophy to be won.
you win this game by loving yourself and loving each other.
this is not a race.

believe that you are beautiful, and you have crossed your very own finish line.
nobody is in the running for your own self-love but you.

stop comparing yourself to girls like her.
you are not meant to look like her because you are not her.
you are you.
you are supposed to look like you.

there are no categories here.
no girls like her or girls like you.

there's just a bunch of beautiful girls.

don't you dare blame me

you tell me
that i hurt you

and i tell you
that i know.

i know i had
a part in this.

we weren't
a one-way street.

but i also know that
i am sitting here,
writing this poem,
and dozens of others,
and you are not even
thinking about me.

i know that
i am sitting here,
barely stitched back together,
and you have hardly given
the scars you left a second thought.

i know that
i am sitting here,
still hurting,
and you are doing
just
fine.

at the root of this

i had only wanted
you to love me
right.

i just wish
you had figured out
how.

realization

i figured out
that it wasn't anything
i did when i met
the other girls you'd
dragged alongside me.

i was never anything
special to you.

i was just another
person for you
to ruin
and leave
behind.

forgive and forget

you ask me
if i can just forgive you
for the bruises
and the scars
and the wounds that still bleed sometimes
that are bleeding now
you tell me
you're sorry
and look the other way
as you say it

i narrow my eyes
and i respond
here's the thing
i don't owe you forgiveness
i don't owe you acceptance
of an apology that i know
doesn't mean a fucking thing
i don't have to forgive you
when i know my forgiveness
is not what you really want

you just want the poems to stop
you just want me to forget about you

but i can't just forget two years of my life
i can't just forget somebody who's left their mark
all over me like a tattoo

so i will write the poetry
and i will write entire books about you
until one day i will be able to forgive and forget you
because i'm healed enough
and not because
you begged me to

you were supposed to be here

i don't understand
this crack between us
that seems to be growing
wider and wider each day,
and i don't know what made you
change your mind.

but i do know this:
you made a promise.

and i know that
this was not supposed
to happen
to us.

i have to learn to be okay with this

people are not meant
to be here forever.
they are only meant to
stick around
for as long as they're
supposed to.

i guess that means it's alright
that i didn't try harder
to make you
stay.

this is the saddest part of healing

i think i have finally
managed to start
hating you.

i think i mean it
when i write it down.

it's not just a coping method
anymore.

and that is what hurts the most,
now.

i used to just think about
forgiving you,
but that felt too much like
loving you,
and that felt too much like
choking on my own breath,
which felt too much like
fucking dying.

so i have to hate you.
i have to loathe you,
at least for a while.

maybe i won't have to
one day.
maybe i will be able to
smile at you and it will be
genuine and kind
and not pulled apart
by a needle and thread.

but for now,
i have to write the angry
poetry and the bitter prose
and i have to want to vomit

at the thought of ever talking
to you again and i have to
ignore you and act like
you don't exist
so that one day

it won't matter that you do.

and i will burn
every memory of you
to ash
until i forget the fire
you ignited
in me

matchstick

i know that
i lit my own matches
and burned down
pieces of us, too.

i haven't forgotten that.

it's just that where i was
a flicker,
you were an entire
inferno.

i am managing

1. you are the first person i want to write about, even now. i could spend hours scribbling out shaky sentences about you and your wolf grin. it's like i enjoy self-sabotage; you are the one thing i don't want to think about, but the only thing i can. i guess this may just be how the brain works.

2. for so long, the poetry felt like a gift for you. look at this, it seemed to cry, look at me still thinking about you. does that make you happy that you're still my muse? i want to say that now it is a gift for myself and my battered heart. it is how i let the pain out so it doesn't kill me.

3. last week, when your username flashed across my screen, i had an anxiety attack. i hadn't spoken to you in months. it made me realize that i had forgotten about you long enough for a reminder to make my hands shake and my throat clench. but i had forgotten, and that's what matters.

4. the thought of seeing you again doesn't make me want to throw up anymore. that doesn't mean i won't vomit when you show up, but at least i'm not crouching over a toilet at the idea of it.

5. i used to say you were toxic. it took me a long time to realize you had been more than just a bout of food poisoning. you were like too much to drink. you were like the robber smashing through my bedroom window. you were like the monster under the bed. you left me shaken and scared to touch a glass. to leave the window cracked on a hot night. to go to sleep without checking behind my bed skirt.

6. you were abusive. and i think i had been saying you were without really realizing it. i think it took a lot longer for the after of us to hit than i thought it would. i thought the worst of it had passed, but i was wrong. the worst of it is here, now. because this is the happiest i've

been and it's because you're not here and that, that is
why. i thought you would be here for this. i didn't think
it would be because you're not.

7. but i can say it now. i can say you were abusive and
there's a weight behind it. i don't just say it in my poetry
because i think it sounds more powerful. now, i say it
because i can't *not* say it. i can't ignore it when it spends
its time staring me in the face. i have to face it, i think. i
have to say it enough times so that eventually, i can
acknowledge the storm you brought to me without
wanting to find shelter. eventually, i will no longer even
feel the rain.

when i am finished healing / things you find in your grandparents' basement

there were good parts of us.
of you.
i will always be the first
to admit that.

and sometimes,
i find myself picking through our memories
like old antiques you find in your grandparents' basement.
sometimes, i blow off the dust on the day we met,
or the first time we kissed.
i wipe the dirt from the moment i realized
that i was in love with you,
and the first time i said it out loud.

i flip through our best times
like old photo albums,
listen to your laughter
like it's a dusty vinyl record.

but i always end up sitting in front of
the chipped china plates in the corner.
the broken picture frames lining the shelves:
our first fight, the first promise broken,
and then lie, after lie, after lie.
crack, after crack, after crack.

i come back to the broken parts
of us because i am not ready
to acknowledge the good parts
by themselves.

i can't trust myself to not stare
at the shiny pieces for too long,
to not forget about the chips and cracks
on the other side of the room.

one day, i won't need to hold
all our shattered pieces in my hand
to know that they're there,
that they aren't going away.
one day, i will be able to
put the record of your laugh on play
without being afraid of forgetting
how that laugh also broke my heart.

one day, i will be able to sit there,
and just listen.

scar tissue

there are permanent marker stains on my blouse / you think i would recognize / your handwriting / but it's smeared from the wash / how many times have i tried to wash you off / how many times will i fail to do so

but i don't mean the silk blouse i wore / on our first date / i mean / the clothes i wear daily / i mean / my skin / i don't mean sharpie / i mean / the scars you left / i mean / when i look at the scar tissue / i am amazed at how it is still pink / at how even now / it still isn't healed / when he touches them / they burn / like somehow / somewhere / you feel it / like you know there are hands on me / and they aren't yours / like for some reason / you still think you deserve / to be the one / like you still think / i'm yours

there are permanent marker stains on my blouse / and i know it's your handwriting / i always have / no amount of wash cycles could erase your signature / out of my head / the scar tissue is still pink / it still burns / i mean / i am still hurting / i mean / i am doing better / i mean / but there is still pain to be endured / i mean / he touches me / and i let it burn / if that means / one day / those scars won't make me feel / anything / at all

ash

after the first time you touched me,
like really touched me,
i told you i burned under your fingertips.

you had looked surprised, worried even,
but i assured you it was a good kind of burn.

the kind of burn like hot coffee sliding down your throat
on a cold winter morning.
the kind of burn like ripping away old skin
to reveal the new underneath.

the kind of scorching a crop gets when they clear the field
for the next harvest.
the kind of scorching that makes it possible for something
new to grow.

cadential

our song sounds like
butterfly wings.
like tongues scraping
against the inside of
a mouth that isn't theirs.

in the morning
i wake up to your heartbeat.
i feel your fingers tapping out
a rhythm on my hipbones.

you are my final cadence.
the last chord after years
of halves.

bloom

i first knew i was in love with you
when we were laying in my bed
and my fairy lights were twinkling
over us, and i was resting my head
on your chest and you were tracing circles
across my back with your fingers,
and you were explaining to me the origins
of kissing.

"it was actually a feeding mechanism," you said,
and then you laughed, and i knew i was in love with you
right then, at that moment, but it was too early to tell you.
still too early to tell myself, even.
but that was when i knew.
because when you laughed, the gears in my heart slowed
and suddenly began cranking back in the right direction.

i spent a lot of time kissing you instead of saying it.
when i felt the words pressing against the back of my teeth
i would distract myself with your mouth.
and i think i was afraid, not because i didn't think you would say
it back, but because this time i wanted it to be right.

every time before i've dived headfirst into their chests,
wrapped my fingers around their hearts too quickly, too roughly.
i would spit out that i loved them so they would have some sort
of anchor to me, some sort of tie, some sort of seed that would
hopefully sprout into something requited.

but with you, i held it in. stapled my lips shut with my own
hands in an effort to get this time right, to make this time work. i
would not try and make us grow before we had put the roots
down deep enough. i would not try and make us bloom before it
was time.

it was when we were skin on mouths on tongues on hands
that i told you. at the peak of everything unspoken,

i broke the silence, and i can still remember the exact words i said: "i love you, and you may not be sure yet, but i am, so," and when you said it back, just seconds later, it was like i didn't even need to feel worried in the first place. of course you do. of course. but i like to think it was because i let us blossom on our own.

darling, you are the one thing in my life
i want so desperately to just make it.
i want us, through everything.
you and everything, everything and you.
not need, no. i would survive,
but you are something
i don't feel selfish for wanting so badly.
you are something that doesn't make
me feel bad for being so greedy.

past or present

i loved him with jagged nails
and broken teeth,
in between the maybe and the already gone.

he was gone before i ever arrived,
and i think i was in love with a ghost,
or a shadow, or a nightmare.

i love you with ruby red lips
and soft hands,
right in the center of the now.

you were here when i showed up,
and i think you may have been waiting for me,
or i am just so used to loving a phantom
that i could hardly believe you were real.

i can't change this

i do not know
if there will come a time
where i am totally okay again.

i think i am always going
to be paralyzingly paranoid
about every little thing.

i think i am always going
to find a syllable to doubt
in somebody's sentence.

i have learned many things
over these past few years.

and the most important of them all,
is that the battle is not
fighting to not be that way.

the battle is being that way
and fighting to accept it.

bone shatter

i figured out that we were poisoning each other when i realized
we are more bite than bark, always more teeth than tongue,
sharp and to the point. never louder than we need to be.
there were no soft blows in our fights, only hard, back-breaking
ones.

and i wanted that.
i wanted some sort of love that would break my bones
over and over again.

something that would leave me reeling.

but i think, now, that maybe there's a reason for all of this.
maybe i am not meant to be another chewed-up lover of yours.

it takes courage to realize that pain and love
don't always have to be synonymous.

sometimes, you can just take love
and run with it.

i have learned
how to wrap my heart
in barbed wire.

i know how to fortify
its walls with stone,
to keep my castle
safe and sacred.

i am starting
to figure out
who i should let in
and who i should keep

                          out.

eventually,
i will be able
to prevent my heart
from ever breaking
again.

a daily reminder

there will always be good things. remember them. remember
how the sun felt on your skin, remember how good it felt when
they kissed you (or when they didn't). remember that you are
still growing, your flowers are only beginning to bloom. none of
the petals are ready to fall off yet, so don't pick them off because
you don't think you are beautiful enough for them. remember
that your heart is only a muscle. muscles will hurt when
overworked, so maybe you shouldn't always love so much.
remember that it's okay to wear red lipstick and tight dresses and
high heels and raise a middle finger to the world because anyone
who cares if you're holding your head high is holding their head
far too low to see the twinkle in your eyes. remember that tears
aren't always bad. sometimes, sadness opens your eyes to the
truth about everything. you won't move mountains or split the
sea but you can move people's minds and split hearts in two, and
maybe, that's all the change you need to make.

medicine

hidden behind
my skeleton cage lies a heart.
it beats despite the weight it carries.
it beats despite the scars it bears.

for the sake of poetry,
i want to say it has kept beating
so that i could meet you.

but for the sake of honesty,
i know that that is not true.

it kept beating because
it had to.

broken as it may have been,
i gave it no choice.

so it pounded through the pain,
beat through the brutality,
and became stronger.

today it grows stronger, still.

i don't think it kept beating
so that i could meet you.

but i do think that
you are the medicine
it needed to finally
heal its wounds.

glow

i don't think i've ever felt
this sort of pull.

i could spend
an eternity right here,
drawn to you like moths
to flame.

how the words come

let me tell you how
i write.

when my grandparents
read my book for the first time,
they called me asking me if i was sad.

i remember a time when i would have said yes.
would have told them that the bloody imagery
and the gaping pit oozing metaphors was a mirror
of how i feel all the time.

but today, i smile.
today, i laugh at such an idea—
me, sad.
me, not over you.
me, broken.

you see, there's a small part of me
that is just that—
sad, broken, not over you (etc.)
but it is barely a chip of my heart.
a lone dust particle floating in clean air.

when i want to write about you
like you still make my lungs feel stapled
to the wall with my rib cage,
like you still have your claws sunk into my stomach,
i visit this place.

it is dark there.
there is no light switch i can flip on when i enter,
though maybe that is for the best.
if it were light i may be forced to see your face.
but when i walk in, i can hear your laughter.
i take a seat on the ground
and i can feel your hand brushing away my hair.
i let the nausea flood my throat

and i let the tears flow
and i grab the pen.

i let what now is an ounce of hurt
grow again until it weighs enough to crush me
like it once did.

when the poem ends,
i stand up and swallow the pain
down,
down,
down,
until i am once again smiling,
once again laughing
at the notion of the monster you were.

i lock the door when i leave.
put the key in my pocket.

i do not know if i will ever be able
to throw it away.

empty

my old muse
is dying.

i am trying
to pull poetry
from his flesh

but i am struggling
to find anything
in there left for me.

perhaps this is
a sign that there
is nothing left for me
with him at all.

i swear i am trying
my hardest to forget you.

i swear one day
it won't break my heart
to hear your name.

how painful it is,
to realize you were only
temporary
to someone you saw as
permanent.

people say i write best about love: about breakings / buildings / blossoming's / bleedings.

there's a stigma around love poetry that makes it laughable. they say, i have no interest in reading a teenage girl's diary. they say, love poetry is laughable.

like being honest on paper is laughable / like being a teenage girl is laughable / like poetry is laughable

but i am a / teenage girl /

and i don't know love just because of pink-lipped boys and bitterness and a stained memory. i know love in performing on a stage / hitting the perfect chord / realizing what you're doing is what you're meant to be doing. i know love in friendships that never break / sun sweet laughter in moonlit conversations / red wine teeth. i don't know heartbreak just because of text message break ups and five-hour drives and laundry piles of dishonesty. i know heartbreak in my father realizing his dad didn't recognize him anymore / holding my cat as we put him down / leaving my high school choir. i know heartbreak in losing my friends to drugs / reading about mass shootings in the news / not knowing how to help somebody when they need it.

but i am a / teenage girl / so how would i know these things?

is the limit of my emotion dependent on failed relationships / getting cheated on / being called ugly?

or is that just what you want us to think it is?
because you're afraid of what will happen when we realize that you're wrong?

my mother taught me
to be
strong
loud
demanding

to grab attention
by its throat
to turn heads and ears
to make them
listen to me

i will never apologize
for being a force
of nature

i will never apologize
for being the woman
i was raised
to be

women are learning
to stand.

to rip the stitches
you have sewn through
our lips
out.

to speak.
scream.
destroy.

it's time to take back
what you fucking
took from us.

so this isn't a poem.

this is a battle cry.

i don't want to be afraid of you but i have to be

i wasn't raised to be scared of you,
it was just pounded into me every time
i saw another story on the news:

another woman beaten to death
by an ex-lover,
another mother shot
by an abusive husband,
another girl murdered for saying no
to an angry young man.

it's not all men, no,
but it's enough.

it's enough to make us
clutch keys in between our fingers.
it's enough to make us
give out fake numbers instead of saying no.

it's enough to make us
always be ready to run,
to have our friends track our location on dates.

it's enough to make us
feel like we are not our own,
like we do not belong to ourselves.

but eventually you will hear us,
and we won't have to scream
our throats raw to get your attention,
and you will raise your sons to know
what you may not have learned
until you were older, what some of your peers
may never have learned at all:

that we are our own people,
that we do not owe you anything:
not a date, not a number, not a conversation.

that we are not your property and

we do not belong to you.

goddess

my body is not
a monster.

my body is not
to be hidden under beds
or behind closed doors,

my body is not
something society
should be afraid of.

my body is its own
planet.

it has rolling hills
and dimpled craters,
arching mountains
and darkened caverns.

my body has its own
sky;
glittering in my gaze
is its version of a starry night.

learn how to love me right,
and you can scoop entire
oceans out of me.

love me wrong,
and my sky becomes
a thunderstorm.

i am my own
home.

i know no terrain
better than my skin,
can climb no mountain

better than the rise and fall
of my torso.

there is no greater
celestial being,
no stronger goddess,
than a woman who knows
her own worth,
who finds herself
to be ethereal.

perhaps that is why
you have tried so hard
to shut us away.

i should not have to
rip my own voice
to pieces for you
to hear me:

we are not yours.
we have never been yours.

i will never understand
the desire to
rip the steering wheel
from women's hands

do you honestly think
you know us better
than we know ourselves?

do you really believe
you understand our
skin
bones
hearts
souls
better than we do?

how arrogant
how foolish
how *wrong*
of you

to think
you can run
my body
for me

women have spent centuries
having our bodies and value
ranked by men

it is about damn time
we took ourselves back

music is my sanctuary.
i find peace in its melodies
and rhythms.

it is crawling into
a soft warm bed
after a long day.

it is the breath of fresh air
i need after walking
through clouds of smoke.

i hate seeing people shrink
in on themselves.

how desperately
i want to shake
their souls awake.

how badly
i want to tell them,

you are worth it.
i promise you're worth
seeing.

2019

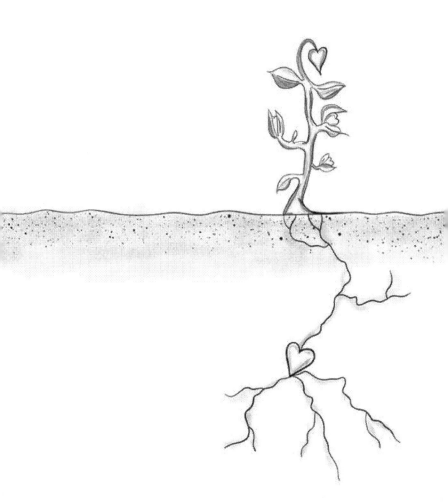

i remember the day i saw the notre dame cathedral / its spire reaching towards heaven / we were supposed to sing there / in three weeks we were supposed to sing there / i remember when i saw it / i said to myself / i want to sing there / so our director says we're going to paris and that we'll get to sing in notre dame and the whole choir weeps / and then it catches on fire / and then we sit and watch the updates and watch that grasping spire crumble in on itself / the roof caving in like the soul of somebody who stopped seeing god in everything he'd been in before / and i thought to myself / how fucked up is this / i thought to myself / we were supposed to sing there / you see / i am not a religious person / never have been / i didn't go to church / and i still don't unless i'm singing / which is fitting because / well / music is the only thing that feels like what i think god would feel like to a priest or rabbi / it is the closest thing i have to a religion / so when i sing in a church / it becomes a holy place for me too / it is no longer something foreign / it is no longer something i don't understand / or even fear / i just wanted to sing in the notre dame cathedral / so that maybe when i ask myself / god / are you there / we would sing a chord / and it would reverberate off the stained glass and wooden ceiling / and the echo / the tears on my cheeks / the faces of the crowd / would sound a little bit like / yes / i am

-when notre dame burned

i still find myself finding reasons
to run after you as if
you are trying to get away from me.

but you are always dancing right out of reach,
knowing that if you looked over your shoulder
i would be right there
waiting for you.

like always.

i have waited years
for the memories
to be less poignant,
less inflammatory,

but nothing comes.
nothing fades.
nothing stops.

your presence is as loud
as it was in the beginning,
and i cannot cover my ears
enough to block you out, so—

don't you think
that if i could,
i would bury you?

do you really think
i haven't been working hard
to put all of us
down?

the way i loved you was
all-consuming.

it was why i had
to let
you go.

watching you love her
is like drowning.

when you look at her
i feel like my lungs
have flooded.
when you kiss her
i stop breathing.
i can't find the air
i need.

and when you don't look back at me?
i feel the ocean
swallowing me
completely
whole.

it's ridiculous that i am still hurting and you're doing fucking fine. it's ridiculous that you can laugh about how crazy i am and i will have panic attacks at the thought of you. it's ridiculous that you are walking out of this scratch free and i look like i've been hit by a fucking semi. it's ridiculous that i'm still obsessing over every second we had together, searching for all the signs i missed until you stabbed me in the face with one. it's ridiculous that what happened with us has to carry into all the relationships i've had since like some sort of ghost. it's ridiculous that you meant enough to me that i can't seem to get over this while you don't even think about me anymore. it's ridiculous that i can't just be in love and be happy without you finding some way to ruin it, even in my head. it's all ridiculous. this should not be my fucking burden to carry, but it is, because the broken always get the short end of the stick. you can see me and smile like i'm a fond memory. that's ridiculous. you should see me and run. you should be afraid to see the mess you've made. but you don't. you never do. you're eager to hear how i am. you want to see all the cracks and count all the missing pieces. and i sit here and let you. every time. and that's ridiculous. i know better but i still let you. i can't tell if that makes me pathetic or if that makes you evil. i think it is a combination of both. still, ridiculous.

it's ridiculous that you broke me like this. it's ridiculous that you meant to.

i was a rest stop
in your life—

i was never meant
to be the
final destination

for when you feel your first heartbreak coming

i've fallen in love
with a lot of people
who didn't know
how to love me back.

i've poured my soul
into relationships
that were never going
to work,

i've given my all
to somebody
who couldn't even
give me a fraction,

and it fucked me up.

being underappreciated
fucked me up.
being lied to
fucked me up.
being cheated on
fucked me up.
being left
fucked me up.

being broken
into a thousand pieces
fucked
me
up.

but despite it all,
i don't regret my pain.
i regret that i thought
it was the end of the world.
i regret that i let myself
sit with something so

loud and ugly for so long.
i regret that i let it tell me
what i was worthy of.
i regret that i believed it.
but i wouldn't take it back.
i needed it to grow.

so do not be afraid
of the heartbreak
that awaits you.

it isn't the end.

the grass is so much
greener here on the
other side,
and the ones here
are just as fucked up,
and just as beautiful,
as you.

and you'll think you're doing fine until you hear their name brought up in conversation and you have to stitch a smile on your face while your stomach plummets out of your body and through the floor. until you have a dream about them and they still love you and you wake up crying and you hit yourself because you were fine, you were surviving and you were getting through it. until an old friend you haven't seen in a few months spots you at the store and the first thing they ask is, "how are you two?" and you have to tell them that it's not two anymore and laugh it off like it's perfectly okay, like you're over it, but you're clenching your fist in your pocket so hard your palm bleeds. you'll think you're not hurting anymore until you're cleaning out your nightstand and you find an old photo of the two of you and the next thing you know you're crying and you want to call them so fucking badly but you know they've changed their number because you've tried before. until you're walking down the street and suddenly you smell something that reminds you of their hair or their clothes and then you can remember everything, from the way their eyes lit up when they talked about their favorite music to the taste of their skin and their tongue and you'll think you're doing fine until you can't go anywhere without thinking you see them around every corner, in every store. until you can't sleep without your dreams turning to nightmares of better times. until you realize you're not fine at all, until you realize you've never been fine, you've never been over it. until you realize you still miss them more than anything. until you realize you still love them.

the cruelest act of cowardice:

the odds were stacked against us
and you were too scared
to try and climb them

here's a reminder that i miss you. i know you don't want to hear it but i'm shouting it anyway. hoping it will reach you. hoping you won't keep covering your ears. hoping that for one second you will care. so i'll say it again: i miss you. please come back. i put everything into our love and i'm watching it wilt. i'm holding crumbling petals in my hands. we could've fixed this. i know we could've. we still can. i love you. come home. the flowers need you.

sweet girl,

this is not the end of you.
he may have been a wrecking ball,
crashing through the home of your heart,
but you are strong.

you are strong,
and you know how to
rebuild.

your heart is only whole once. after that first break, you are just trying to keep those broken pieces glued together. so it's okay to be careful. a little bit selfish. it's okay to clutch it tightly. don't be ashamed of your armor.

20 things i've learned in 20 years

1. look at nature. flowers, blooming at the start of spring. snow falling outside your window. rain drops pounding on your roof. lose yourself in its beauty. love it. protect it.

2. enjoy the little things. getting an extra 30 minutes of sleep. a particularly good cup of coffee. a passing hug or kiss with the people you love. these small moments add up. they're what make life sweet.

3. find an art form and do it. you don't have to be good at it. find your outlet and do it once a day. draw a doodle once a day. write a poem once a day. plunk out a song on the piano once a day. it doesn't have to be perfect. it's art. and i may be biased, but i think one of the most important art forms you can do is:

4. sing. sing in the shower. sing in your car. sing with your friends. sing in a choir. sing by yourself. as my choir director said: music is the international language. it connects us all. if you can sing with someone you can learn to love and understand them.

5. pay attention. don't keep yourself in a bubble. watch the news (the reliable kind). listen to NPR. know what's going on where you live. and if you can: VOTE. your voice MATTERS.

6. stand up for yourself, even if it makes you afraid. if your best friend is being a little too mean with their jokes, tell them. if you know that person said something mean about you? make them say it to your face. this leads to my next thing, which is:

7. sometimes, you have to make people uncomfortable in order to get them to respect you. ask that person why they can't keep your name out of their mouth. call people out on their bigotry. tell somebody to shut the fuck up. but keep in mind that sometimes, the person that needs to be quiet is you, so:

8. know when to shut the fuck up. learn when you need to give your opinion. understand that sometimes, you don't need to be the loudest person in the room, or the smartest. it's not always a competition. you don't always need to 'spill tea' or be shady. not everything needs to be drama. and you don't need to be a part of all of the drama there is.

9. go bare faced. be natural. take selfies with no make-up on. admire how you look in the sunlight. love yourself at your realest and most authentic state. that being said, though:

10. glam yourself up. put on glitter and false eyelashes and blue fucking lipstick and stare at how amazing you look in the mirror. do it for fun. you don't need a reason. have fun.

11. tell people you love them regularly. text them and remind them that they're important to you. they will reciprocate, and if some don't? now you know who your real friends are.

12. sometimes wounds stick around a lot longer than you want them to, a lot longer than you thought they would. it's extremely annoying. but let them bleed and then let them heal. listen to what they're trying to tell you. learn from them. and once they close, don't let them get reopened.

13. i don't know who needs to hear this, but if you're thinking you should leave them: leave them.

14. stop making excuses for other people treating you like shit. it's not your fault. stop telling yourself it's because they're having a bad day. stop saying that you might've stepped on their toes. you don't deserve to be treated like a doormat. you're not a fucking doormat. you're a person. get people to treat you like it.

15. call out bigotry in all forms. it doesn't matter who it is. tell your mom she's being homophobic. tell your uncle he's racist. tell your friend they're supporting rape culture. it's okay to be nice about it, but be firm. don't allow those you love to become part of the problem. those who are silent take the side of the oppressor.

16. don't leave your friends alone at parties. don't let them get so drunk they don't know where they are. keep them away from wandering hands and bad intentions. drag them home if you have to. hold their hair back when they throw up. you'd want somebody there to do the same for you.

17. be naked. sleep naked. lay in your bed after a shower, naked. look at your naked body in the mirror. this is your home. learn to love it. a tip for this is:

18. tell yourself, "i love you," at least three times a day. do it before every meal if you want. do it when you wash your hands in the bathroom. shout it into your pillow. scream it in the middle of your kitchen. even when you don't want to say it, make yourself say it anyway. force it out of your mouth. you'd be surprised how fast you start to believe it.

19. sometimes you'll have to leave people. you'll have to leave homes, relationships, friendships. usually, it's for the best. it always hurts. but know that everything will be okay, because you still have:

20. you. you are your first priority, the one thing in your life, in this world, that you can count on. you will always be there. so take care of yourself. smile more. treat yourself right. get help when you need it. if you take one thing away from this, let it be that. you are meant to be here, and you are so much more than you know.

can you
just
hold on
to me?

i don't like the thought
of being forgotten,

especially when i,
the poet,
the one with words anchored
to my feet,
will never be able
to forget you.

there will always be
another poem
waiting around
the corner.

this is my curse.
bear it with me.

she was stronger
than she let on.

she hid her fierceness,
afraid they would run
from her sharp teeth.

but then, she realized:
to be woman and to be mighty
are not opposites—
they are one
at the same.

i always told myself
i would be ready
when i lost you

that i would not let myself
succumb to the pain

but you're never ready
for heartbreak

you can see it coming
see it raise the hammer

but when your heart shatters
the pain is just as bad
as it would be
if you never thought about it
at all

and this
is the painful truth
of love

sometimes i think about
the love i used to have.

i think i've written enough
about it so i'll keep the words
to myself just this once.

you already know what
i would say anyway,
because it's what
i always do.

all i'll say is—
well—

i hate
to have to wonder but—

do you miss me
from where
             you are?

-just a question

i want to know how
a good love feels on
my skin.

i want to find someone
who can show me.

purge

heartbreak to me nowadays
is more of a bloody shock,
a grisly purging.
it is the shaking realization
that you have to leave somebody—
not today, not tomorrow,
but someday.

heartbreak feels like
the panic attack
you have in the bathroom at work
when it hits you that there's
an expiration date, here,
and it's loud and bright
and very not up for discussion,
it's not exact, there's no written
day or time,
but it just says
end.
and you know.

i am not somebody
who ignores things,
and when i realized i was
falling out of love with you
it was not something
i could swallow down.
i had felt it climbing
up my throat for weeks
and had been choking
on its black and slimy truth
until i finally just couldn't.
you cannot fight these things
forever.

i think i start missing people
the second they say hello.
i think that i am always preparing

for the end
as soon as we press start.
i think i do this so by the time
it comes, and i am crying
to you in your living room
and our love is crumbling
to pieces in front of you
i am already
okay.

i am already halfway
out the door
and maybe that makes
me heartless but maybe
it is because i love you
too much
to make this messier
than it needs to be.
to tie up all the ends
and push you away
and make sure you know
that it's okay.
it's over and it's done
and i am breathing
and so are you
and i love you still,
so sweetly and tenderly,
but this thing is not
what we need anymore.

and we'll be fine.
i already am.

a poem where i come to terms with being forgotten

i was your first love,
but she was your greatest.
i was those first moments
of flame, the first graze
of sparks against your fingertips,
but she was the lighter
you held against your thumb.
she was everything that made
you feel alive; everything burning,
everything dangerous and looming.

i was your first love,
but she was your first heartbreak.
i was the easy one to leave.
you loved me until you merely didn't
but you loved her until you just couldn't
manage to cough up anything else.
fading is much less painful than breaking
and that's what i did—
i faded. for you, yes, but mostly
for myself. i began to dim the lights
the moment she walked in.
i don't even know if you remember
saying goodbye, if you ever even did.

i was your first love,
but who would have known?
i don't think you remember me
like that. perhaps to you,
i am nothing more than
the girl you held for just shy
of a year, nothing more than a stop
on the way to her.
but to me you were everything.
and for a while i knew that to you,
i was everything too.

i was your first love,

but would you even recognize my face?
or would you look at me and think,
it's weird,
she doesn't look like i remember.

i keep thinking i'll be able
to tell you to leave me be

but i just smile and tell you
i'm doing well
because part of me
still belongs to you

even now.

do you ever think about
what could've happened
if you'd decided to stay?

if you'd wanted
to try and fight for us
the way i wanted to?

do you ever think about
what could've happened
if you had decided

i was worth it?

my body is my canvas
and i will paint it
however i wish.

i don't need your
fucking permission.

the admired man, the hated woman

my mother taught me
how to swallow reality
at a young age.

she told me,

"to be woman
does not mean
to be weak.

to be woman
does not mean
to be less than.

to be woman
does not mean
to be small.

but you live in a world
where many people
think that it does."

i have spent my life
being too much
for a lot of people—

boys would call me too bossy
for taking charge
of a game at recess,
and years later men
would call me the same
for stepping up to do things
that they didn't want to do,
or in many cases,
simply couldn't.

my friends would call me too loud
for being carefree

at the lunch table,
and years later that has transformed
into people speaking down to me
for speaking out—i am now too loud
in a very different way.

people would say i dreamt too big
for a young girl,
but the dreams never left
even as they did,
and now i am living the fantasy
of my 8-year-old self,
and as i prepare to live the one
of my 20-year-old heart,
people call me too ambitious.

so i have spent a lifetime
of being too much.

too bossy.
too loud.
too ambitious.
too know-it-all.
too selfish.

and at the core of it,
i am
too
woman.

because all of these things
are what men are praised for—
our society admires the men who become
politicians and businessmen
and wealthy and successful.
we worship the stories of
millionaires who started with
nothing.

we praise the men who were
bossy
loud
ambitious
know-it-all
selfish.

so tell me,
what is the difference?
what about my headstrong attitude
makes me
bossy and irritating
and not
a natural leader?

what about my big voice (and desire to use it)
makes me
loud and annoying
and not
somebody who speaks their mind?

what about my big dreams
makes me
too ambitious for my own good
and not
somebody with a plan
and the means to
achieve it?

what about my intelligence
makes me an annoying know-it-all
and not
smart?

what about putting myself first
makes me a selfish bitch
and not
somebody who knows they are a priority?

my mother taught me
how to swallow reality
at a young age.

she told me,
"you are everything
an admired man is,
and that makes you
everything a hated woman
is too."

and i think,
as i have grown older,
that nothing could
possibly be
more true
than that.

i am sorry
for all the times
i was difficult to love.

i am trying so hard
to be someone
worth staying with.

i have done nothing to deserve this pain
but i let the wounds bleed—

i like how you smile
when you're hurting me.

vacancy

we had a love that lived here once.

it kept the windows clean
and the tables dusted,

the silverware polished,
the bed made.

now,

i pull myself out of dirty sheets
each morning and trace your name
into the shower grime.

the dishes piled in the sink,
ready to topple.

i find remnants of you
inside empty cabinets:

your hair hiding with the dust bunnies,
your scent dancing in the mildewed pillows.

i don't know when the roof
started to cave in on us,
or when the doors fell from their hinges.

i can't remember what day
it (you) decided to leave,

but the windows have been clouded
ever since.

people leave. they pack their bags and just leave. and you're stuck watching the door swing shut behind them, wondering where you went wrong. i think that wondering, that thinking, is almost worse than them leaving in the first place.

2020

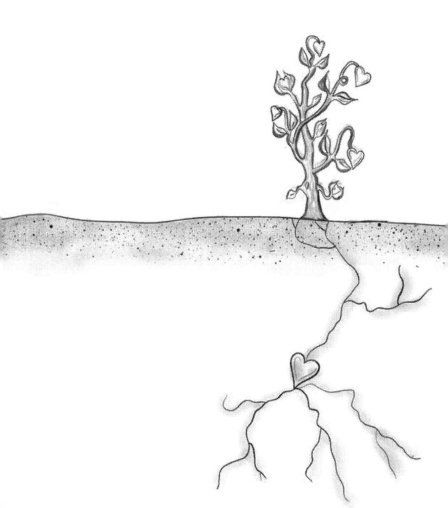

if i could have a choice,
i would choose to have you
back at my side again.

if i could have a choice,
i would choose a life
where i never had to
walk away from you.

you know, i still miss him sometimes. but it's okay. it doesn't hurt like it used to. life is still good even when he creeps back into my mind. i still sleep peacefully even when he shows up in my dreams. i've let it go. i've let *him* go. he's just another ghost, and i can't let him haunt me anymore.

i'm glad you're gone,
but i still miss you, sometimes.

or,
i miss the person
i thought you were.
the person i wanted you to be.

when it comes to you,
most days i am teetering
on the edge between

happiness and sadness.

one day i fall one way,
the next i fall the other.

the sadness was comforting,
something familiar,
which is why i fell towards it
so many times.

but lately i have been leaning
in the opposite direction.

happiness might be unfamiliar,
but there is something warm
about experiencing something

new.

you made me feel as though
i was too much,
that nobody could ever love
all of me.

but the truth is that
you simply didn't want
to take the time to.

you broke my heart
and i still don't know
what was worse—

that you called it love
or that i believed you.

i write about you a lot
during the summer,
ripping stitches out of old wounds,
using the blood as ink.

i think what i'm trying to say is:

this is the one time of year
where i miss you loudly
and i can understand it.

this is the one time of year
when everything reaches for you,
straining against tired skin,
and i let it.

this is the one time of year
when it all hurts,
and i know exactly why.

there's a world i visit
every night before bed.

in it,
i do not know
your name.

it bounces
around me softly,
no longer sharp or pointed,
unable to hurt me
any longer.

as i drift
off to sleep
and inevitably
see you there,
i long for
this world's
embrace.

i long for
the world
where your name
is just that—a name,
and not
a knife buried
deep into my chest,
twisting with every
letter.

i did not write when we were together.

writing meant facing the truth.

and i did not know how—
i did not want—
to face the truth of us.

so of course, in this aftermath,
there are too many words to hold.

of course, among all this ruin,
there are thousands of words to find.

i never planned to make a home out of you.
i didn't mean to put my heart in your hands.
it wasn't my intention.
this attachment that has grown from the feeling
of your lips on mine,
the way you looked at me that one time.
i didn't want it, and i know you didn't either.

but thank you, i guess, for trying.
for offering my heart your hospitality
even when it overstayed its welcome,
even when i was no longer able
to be discreet about the fire you lit
in me.
i know you didn't want to feel the warmth
of its flames.
in the end
you didn't love me,
but you tried to.

at least you tried to.

hand jobs in a movie theatre / becoming

when i was in the 9th grade
a girl i didn't know from another school
gave her boyfriend of five seconds a hand job
in a movie theatre because he said he'd love her if she did it.
instead, he texted all his friends and told them
about how she was so eager to get her hands
on him while she went to the bathroom to
wash them off and by the time she got back
half the grade knew and her phone was
exploding with things like,

wanna give me one?
i'd like to see what you can do

but most popular were the terms

slut
whore
nasty
disgusting
shameful

and she called her mom to come get her early,
told her that she didn't feel good,
and soon she didn't feel good once a week,
and then it was twice a week,
and then suddenly it was
every single morning.

her mom finally pulled the words from her mouth,
all riddled with bite marks from mean girls
and slime from pervy boys
and she said,
honey why did you do it?

and the girl told her,
he said he would love me.
i mean i don't know exactly how that conversation

went but i just know that halfway through that year
she left and didn't come back.
at least that's what we heard.

so here's another poem about slut-shaming
and how when i was 14 i heard all about how they
ruined the life of a girl when really they should have
been crucifying that fucking boy.
and i always thought that, always wondered about
that loose end, how it was never tied up
quite right for my taste.
because his friends thought he was so cool for it
but also hated her, or maybe they loved her?
and i think the girls in my classes who would
sit and whisper about what a slut she was
loved her, too.
loved her in the ugliest way possible,
loved her in a way that left her completely traumatized,
but i think they loved her for doing it.
because i think we all wanted—just a little bit—to do it,
we just knew what would happen if we did.
so we sat and waited for somebody else to take the fall
and did what we were taught to do:
celebrate and excuse the boy.
ostracize and torture the girl.

we can argue all day about whether or not
14- and 15-year-olds should be giving hand jobs
and you're right to say that they shouldn't
but the point is that they are,
and they're going to keep learning
at a very young age that girls are sexual objects
and boys are meant to take and throw them away,
like leftovers nobody wants,
unless we unearth this notion that sexual history
is what determines your value
and we stop blaming rape on clothes and start blaming the rapist
and men stop asking us to be sexual and then hate us for it
and women—we have to stop hating us for it, too.

i don't know what happened to that girl
but i know that the word *slut* is branded into her skin
and it probably follows her like a ghost whenever
she goes on a date.
i wish i could find her and tell her that i'm sorry.
that she didn't know me but i knew her and
that i knew better even then but i didn't know enough
to open my mouth.

i hope she isn't afraid of the words *i love you*
and i hope she only hears them from people who mean it
and i hope she has forgotten the face of that cruel fucking boy
and all of them. i hope she has forgotten all of them.
if not yet, then one day.

i hope she has a mantra she has taught herself,
and it goes something like this:

my sexual history is not a value meter.
it does not sink every time i kiss somebody new
and it does not rise when i sit happily in a relationship.
if i want to have sex i will have it and i don't give a fuck
what you think about it because you will treat me with respect,
you will treat me like the strong, intelligent woman that i am.
i am deserving of your time.
i am not to be brushed off as somebody less than you
because of an archaic ideal that woman cannot be sexual
because they want to be.
he did not determine my worth.
he did not determine my worth.
he did not determine my worth.

but i don't know if she does.
all i know is that
somewhere out there a young woman sits,
and thousands like her,
haunted by the decision she made
when she was just blooming into herself.
a decision that should not have ruined her

adolescence like it did.

somewhere out there a young man sits,
and thousands like him,
reminiscing on the first time
he got a hand job.

it was when i became a man,
he jokes with his friends.

the young woman sighs,
takes a sip of her wine:

it was when i became
a woman.

i don't know what to think of you

at night i tell the stars about you
because maybe they'll
understand what it means
to be surrounded
by such light

and maybe they also know
that some things are long gone
way before that light dies out

i will never forget the way
you looked when i told you
i was leaving.

the way your cheeks
drained of their color,
the way your lip trembled,
the way your eyes widened
and misted over with tears.

you might not believe it,
but that moment haunts me
more than you will ever know.

because
i may not have loved you
the way you wanted—
enough to stay—
but i did love you enough
to know that it was time
to walk away.
that remaining by your side
when i longed to be elsewhere
was only going to hurt you
even more.

you may never understand that,
and i can't do anything about it,
other than tell you that
i, too, wish it could've been different,
and i never wanted this to happen, either.

i wanted to see the world with you,
not open the door for us and be left behind.

(tell me, how does she feel at your side?)

i am so tired
of fighting
to hold onto
a love
that will not
hold me back.

i think the worst thing you did wasn't the lying or the manipulating, it was the way you dismantled all the work i'd done to love myself. before you came along, i saw myself as beautiful, and for the longest time after you left, i didn't.

what is love
without passion?

i used to ask myself that
during moments of doubt
about us.
when things started
feeling wrong,
when your manipulation started
to lose its hold it had on me.

passion is not draining,
passion does not wear you down.

passion can burn,
passion can frighten you,
but passion does not break you.

what is love
without passion?

well, more importantly,
what is love?

certainly not
this.

the other day the sky
looked like one giant bruise

all red and purple
and orange and blue

and i remembered the time
my heart looked like that too

the time when i used to be
so in love with you

in which love is very different yet the same

the first time i fell in love
it left me in the middle of the night,
didn't so much as leave a note behind,
and i sat on the couch
and waited for its return.

when it walked in through the door months later
i felt nothing but relief,
even though it looked different now—
it was sadder, angrier, it spoke to me
with a sharper tongue,
and eventually it left too.
that was the second time.

when love came home to me again,
it was gentle, soft. i basked in its warmth.
but it wasn't enough.
i don't know why it wasn't enough.
the third time, i was the one who kicked
love out.

but love didn't stay away for long this time,
it came barreling back through the door
just days later, beautiful and cruel.
it held me by the throat and kissed me hard
and i couldn't tell if the reason i couldn't breathe
was because of its hands or its lips.
in the end, it was both, and that was why
i let it stay so long.
in the end, i was the one who left.

i wandered into the home of the fifth,
and love held me there once more,
helped me regain my footing.
i found a new place to call my own,
no cracks in the walls,
and made my home there.
i think love expected me to stay with it,

but i couldn't. its home was not for me.

when love showed up at my door
for the last time, i only cracked it open.
for a while i kept the chain locked in place.
i peered at love through an inch wide gap.
do i risk it? i thought. *is it worth it?*
i opened the door eventually,
and love made its home here,
repainted some of the walls,
moved some of the furniture,
but i like it.
i like it so much, in fact,
that i cannot remember what it looked like
before love arrived.

and love has changed so much, too.
love has aged and darkened and cried
and broke too many times to count.
but love is with me now.
its eyes are a different color from
the first time i answered my door to
its knocking,
but i know them just the same.

i remember our best moments.
all our brilliant, beautiful moments.
sometimes the fact that
i loved you makes no sense,
and on those days
our best moments keep me company.

they say,
do you remember this?
they say,
we had it all, once.

i say,
yeah.
yeah, we did.

what i told myself in those first 24 hours:
it'll be okay.

it'll be okay.

we had to do it.

i miss you.

i shouldn't have done it.

i should've let us have more time.

it'll be okay.

i'm so sorry.

i'll come back to you.

what happens if you forget me?

what happens if i forget you?

please don't forget me.

i just let the love of my life go.

we had to do it.

it'll be okay.

one day this won't hurt as much.

i miss you.

i shouldn't have said anything.

i needed to say something.

i felt it in my gut. doesn't make it any easier, but...

i don't know how to do this without you.

that's why this needed to happen.

i need to know how to do this without you.

you need to know how to do this without me.

i have to make this worth it.

if this is it, i have to make this worth it.

if it's meant to be, it will be.

it'll be okay.

we had to do it.

i love you, still.

we'll make it.

it'll be okay.

i thought knowing it was coming would make it easier. it didn't.

i'm so sorry.

when i woke up i forgot and for a moment i was happy.

when i remembered it, i tried my hardest to hold on to the happy part.

this isn't the end for us. it can't be.

but what if it is?
it'll be okay.
if it's the end then thank you.
if it's the end then maybe in our next life.

you say
i mean
i tell my friends
that i love them
with a smile

and so we say
love you—
as a friend

and say
the truth
with our eyes

i am terrified of being
the one who gets forgotten.
i have been the one who forgets—
i always have been,
and even then, it still stings
when they finally stop looking
back over their shoulder
and start looking forward
towards somebody else.
i still wince when the door
finally closes.

so i am terrified of being
forgotten by you.
i am terrified that
i will be waiting
for somebody who won't
come back.
i am terrified that
i will watch you fall in love
with somebody else,
and i will be stuck
thinking that i made the worst
mistake of my life in letting you go,
even if it was what had to happen.
even if it was the best choice.
i am terrified that
one day i will reach for you,
and nobody
is going to be there.

i remember listening to the rain
and tracing your collarbone
with my mouth
and everything was perfect,
and everything that could have hurt me
was gone.

now the rain hits the window
and i lie in bed alone
and your lips are a ghost.
this love is a phantom
hovering in the corner.

but i would rather be haunted
than have to watch it fade away.
i would rather sit with this
sad company
than face an empty room.

it's the moments
where i feel like
i'm losing you
where i realize how
important you are.

they always say
you never realize
how good something is
until it's gone.

i don't want
to realize how good
you are when it's too late.

but in the moments
where i think we may
never speak again,
i sit with the possibility
that this is it for us
and the panic
that rises up in me
is so large it takes up
all the space within me.

life without you
for a while
is necessary.
valuable.

but life without you
forever
is horrifying.

this is not a goodbye

it's occurred to me that i don't know who i am if i'm not either in love or falling into it. the most pivotal periods of my life have been tied to another person being there to experience them with me. in many ways, i am lost when there is not somebody by my side. i have bounced from one love to the next for years. all have been thrilling in their own ways but only twice has it been the kind of love where i felt as if it could be my last. the first broke me. the second brought me to life in a way i never could have imagined. you.

i think i am addicted to the feeling of falling for somebody, the adrenaline that accompanies every first, so in that way i know that i will not be stuck in this feeling of loneliness forever. i will find somebody who will make my heart pound again. i may even convince myself that i love them. but i doubt that it will come close to what i have had to walk away from and will hopefully come back to someday. it will maybe ease the ache and take up the time waiting for the stars to line up again. maybe i will even forget, for a fleeting moment, and believe i have found someone who could fill in the missing pieces. it wouldn't be the first time it's happened, but i know it always comes to an end.

however, i think, first, i would like to know myself not through somebody else's eyes. i would like to fall in love with myself. it's not that i haven't loved myself—i do, and i have, for a long time. but while i haven't placed my worth in somebody's hands for years, i have placed my experiences there. every moment of joy, of anger, of sadness, i've shared with somebody. every life-changing moment has been split between somebody else and me. because i loved them. because i wanted them to be there for it.

and i still want that. i still want you to be there for these things. you are in every vision of my future. but i cannot keep you right now, nor can you keep me. so i have no desire to fall in love again. i feel no need to find the next big romance, the next person to sweep me off my feet. i am realizing that i need to learn how to be alone. not entirely. but how to only be surrounded by friends, and maybe a lover at times, but not a love. how to be happy with life even if i am separated from my future. it may be the hardest, but most necessary, lesson i'll ever have to learn.

i am looking toward the future with a mixture of excitement and terror. i am excited because the next chapter of my life is starting. i am terrified because i am entering it without you. i am excited because i know i am sitting on the cusp of great transformation. i am becoming the person i've been dreaming of since i was little. in many ways, all of my dreams are coming true. but i am terrified because what if the person i am meant to be is one that is not meant to be with you? what if, during this period, you realize the same for yourself? how would we handle that realization? will we just drift apart slowly and let the promises we made fade away? will we have to say it—*i don't think we were meant for each other, after all.* how would we bury this? how could we?

i don't know who we will be this time a year from now, much less two, three, or four years down the road. we could be dead. we could be with other people. we could have forgotten. hopefully though, we've become the people we always envisioned we would become. and hopefully, that involves being by each other's sides. if not, i'm sure we'll come to peace with that if we haven't already. if not, i'm sure everything will happen just the way it's meant to. if not, i am sure that i will always look back to you with nothing but love and gratitude in my heart.

2021

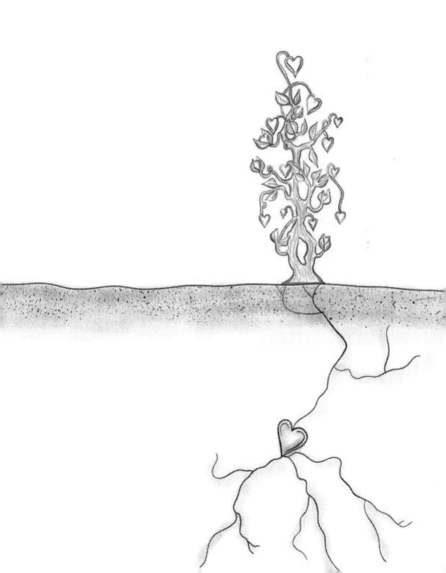

sometimes, you may think something is right person, wrong time. but not everything that comes to an end is meant to be started again. sometimes, they are just the wrong person. and you are not wrong for loving them, or for wanting more time, but when you look back on them in five years, you'll understand that some loves are meant to last for just awhile, not forever.

when i think of you now,
i no longer see the future
we once dreamed of.

i supposed that is
both reassuring and heartbreaking,
both optimistic and mournful.

i hope they make you happy. happy enough to want to take the time to learn how to treat them. happy enough to not break them like you broke me.

i'm stuck in a world of

maybes,

where what ifs grow like trees,
and possibilities bloom like flowers.

where
maybe you didn't kiss me
when you didn't really mean it.

where
maybe i was able to run
when i should have.

where
maybe i loved you
and it was enough.

if only
it had been
enough.

i wonder how long i will miss you.
how long your voice will haunt me
before it fades into background noise.

i wonder how long i will feel as though
i need you even though i don't,
like life without you feels like
looking at the world
through a lens of gray.

i wonder how long i will ask myself,
"is there a way this could have worked?"
i wonder how many times i will run through
all the possibilities before i realize
that there wasn't.

i guess the worst thing now
is that i have to love you silently—
i can't yell it in the streets
or let you know whenever
i feel like it anymore.
i can only scream it to
the barriers of my mind.

eventually, it will fade
away into a faint hum.
i will grow so used to
its buzz that i won't even
notice it until someone asks
about you or i meet someone
with your name or we run into
each other in the grocery store.
only then will it grow so loud
i can't think of anything else.

some people say it will go silent
completely—that one day i'll see you
and there won't even be a whisper,
but i know better.

i wrote once that
i could live without you,
but that i didn't want to have to.

well,
now i have to.

at least
for a little while.

i am so deathly afraid
that the next time our eyes meet
you will find yourself staring
at a stranger and i will find myself
watching somebody realize
that i have become a person
they no longer recognize.

i know you probably won't ever forgive me
and that's okay. it's okay.
i don't know if i deserve it, anyway.
but i meant every word i said.
i did believe. i promise.
part of me always will.

tell me
there's a universe
where this works.

tell me
there are versions of ourselves
existing that are pressed heart to heart,
with nothing standing in their way.

tell me
there's a me and a you
out there somewhere
that have places
to put all this
fucking want.

maybe one day
it won't be so hard
to look at you
and think of
all the love
that could have
been here.

all the love
that was already
taking root,
wrapping its
vines around
my rib cage.

it's a shame your name
is so common,
it's so miserable
the way it's going to
wash over me every time
i hear it fall from another
person's mouth.

i said i wasn't the kind of person
to let love eat me alive,
but then i met you.

now, i am
all *devour me in my entirety,*
all jumping into its mouth
headfirst with my arms outstretched.

the end isn't even close
but i'm already grieving
all the moments we won't
get to share.
already preparing for
all the longing that
is waiting for me
when we run out of time.

what do you want?
you ask, tongue
pressed up against my teeth,
hands molding into the flesh
of my thighs,

and i almost say,
i want this to work.
i want you, forever,
waking up next to me
each morning, kissing
my forehead before you
go and make coffee.

i almost say,
i would marry you
right now if you asked me,
and i'd tell everyone else
to get the fuck over it.
i want things to be this easy
for the rest of my life.
i want nothing but this,
your soft smiles
and gentle fingers
and the way you
say my name in all lowercase,
like it's the most delicate thing
in the world, every time.

i almost say,
i want this love,
not something like it,
but this love, specifically,
until i grow old and die happy
because i had you and you had me
and it worked. it was easy and it worked
and there wasn't something out
of our control that meant it couldn't.
that's what i want, the only thing i'll ever want.

but i just say,
you,
instead, and hope
that it gets the point across.

how many new things
will you show me
before this ends,
how many songs
and moments and places
will we share before
this is over?

how many ways
will you change me
for the better before
we have to say goodbye;
how many parts of me
will bear your mark
when this is done?

in the end,
how much of myself
will simply be pieces
of you?

i once hated the way your ghost haunted me.

now, i laugh in its face.

look at all i've done without you, i say.

look at all the beauty that has been born from the ruin you left me in.

about the author

Catarine Hancock is a 22-year-old poet and opera singer from Lexington, Kentucky. She holds a Bachelor of Music in Vocal Performance from the University of Kentucky and is currently earning her Master of Music in Voice at Indiana University. Aside from music, poetry is her other great love. Having been a bookworm and writer all her life, her passion for poetry began at the age of 13, and shortly after she began sharing her writing online. Over the next 9 years, her platform has grown to an audience of over 300,000. She is the author of three other poetry collections: *shades of lovers* (2020), *sometimes i fall asleep thinking about you* (2021), and *i gave myself the world* (2023), all published with Central Avenue Publishing. When she is not singing or writing, Catarine can be found curled up with a good fantasy novel, wandering the aisles of the local bookstore, or adding a weird décor item she found at Goodwill to her already too-cluttered apartment.

You can find Catarine on social media here:
TikTok: @catarinehancock
Instagram: @catarinehancock
Twitter: @writingbych

about the artist

Abigail Brannon is a 19-year-old artist from Atlanta, Georgia. She is currently a student at the University of Kentucky, where she studies Writing, Rhetoric, and Digital Studies. She expresses her creativity through writing, drawing, and filmmaking, and she also has a radio show called *soundwaves* at wrfl.fm, a local radio station in Lexington.

For inquiries, contact her at abigailbrannon8@gmail.com.